SEX IS HOLY

SEX IS HOLY

MARY ROUSSEAU

&

CHUCK GALLAGHER

AMITY HOUSE
AMITY, NEW YORK

Published by Amity House Inc.
106 Newport Bridge Road
Warwick, N.Y. 10990

Cover Design by Klaboe & Siwek Associates

Library of Congress Cataloging-in-Publication Data

Rousseau, Mary F.
    Sex is holy.

    1. Sex — Religious aspects — Catholic Church.
2. Marriage — Religious aspects — Catholic Church.
3. Catholic Church — Doctrines.   I. Gallagher, Chuck,
1927–   II. Title.
BX1795.S48R69   1986   241.66   86-14188
ISBN 0-916349-11-X

Foreword

by Bernard J. Cooke

Much has been written in recent years about the so-called "sexual revolution". Most of this attention has centered on sexual activity outside of marriage, but it may well be that the most drastic and most lasting shift in attitudes and behavior has to do with the sexual relationships of married couples.

In religious traditions, such as the Roman Catholic, where a relatively clear and strict moral outlook is still maintained, the change in people's understanding of married sexuality has been especially marked. Prior to World War II only the begetting of children was viewed as a goal that thoroughly justified sexual intercourse; and the sexual activity of a married couple, particularly of the woman, was commonly looked upon ethically and religiously as the fulfillment of a contractual duty towards the other partner.

For a variety of reasons, social and religious, this has changed. The emphasis on the human person, upon the importance and human dignity and equality of each individual, which has marked the past few decades, has deeply touched Christian thought about marriage. Vatican II's *Pastoral Constitution on the Church and the Modern World* was grounded in this more personalist understanding of human life and institutions, and no place is this more marked than in its treatment of marriage. While procreation and nurture of children is still viewed as a primary purpose of marriage, there is a new attention paid to the relationship between the spouses and to the family as a community of persons. And the sexual element in the married relationship is seen as fundamental to the relationship and as a positive God-given force for the sanctification of the two persons and their children.

Growth in understanding the relationship between married persons has been aided by recent developmental psychology. The notion that there is a sequence of stages through which a human passes as he or she moves towards adulthood has become commonplace in recent years. And though various explanations of this maturing process differ in their details, there is common agreement that one of the last stages in maturity is the ability to relate honestly and intimately with one's fellow humans. Intimacy is an indispensable ingredient in all mature friendships and most specially in a true love relationship between man and woman. Such personal intimacy is therefore the objective of truly adult sexual activity.

While such developments were taking place in theological and psychological reflection, there was an accompanying growth in grass-roots movements which applied and supplemented these theoretical understandings. The Christian Family Movement and more recent Marriage Encounter — to take but two of the better known examples — have led thousands of Christian couples to a more positive view of their marital sexuality. Yet, as they have begun to appreciate the key role of their sexual relationship in their human development and their Christian sanctification, these couples have felt increasingly a need for deeper theological understanding of human sexuality. Basically what they are seeking is further understanding of the Christian sacramentality of human friendship and of marital sexuality.

This present volume is intended to help fill that need. No one book can, obviously, treat all the various elements in what is a complex area of human experience; but what this book does is to focus honestly and appreciatively on marital sexuality as a key to authentic personal intimacy and on intimacy between husband and wife as a key to sexual maturity. It should provide a two-pronged challenge to Christian reflection. On the one hand it should challenge Christian married couples to understand more deeply and with a truly Christian outlook the sexual dimension of their life together. On the other hand it should challenge theologians to probe more deeply into the insights provided by human sexuality as a metaphorical avenue for understanding the divine.

Present-day Christian theology is being enriched by the use of human experience, and particularly the faith experience of believing communities, as the starting point for theological reflection. Because of its indispensable role in the sacramentality of human life, the experience of friendship, and in particular the paradigm experience of married love, can and should provide an entry into deepened understanding of the mystery of God's saving love in Jesus as the Christ. Christian marriage must come to be effectively sacramental of the saving power of human love and human sexuality.

Contents

To Ed, the third person of our trinity.

Preface

This book is for anyone who wants to make the most of sexual intimacy, which is the heart of the sacrament of matrimony. It is addressed to couples who wish to make good marriages even better. It is also meant for those who guide such couples — priests and psychologists, educators (religious and otherwise), therapists and counselors. It is, in a way, for other professionals, too — sociologists, philosophers, and theologians. It is for social activists, too, and missionaries, for it speaks about the most powerful force the world knows for transforming us human beings and the world that we make for ourselves. All of us are sexual beings. And all of us are deeply influenced by the married couples who touch our lives, both in our families and out of them. The book, then, is really addressed to everyone. For everyone has some kind of stake in making the sexual intimacy of couples more luminous and more effective in lighting the way to the life of love that all of us are called to.

The book has two authors. It is, indeed, a wedding itself: a permanent, loving union of Chuck Gallagher's experience with couples during his years with Worldwide Marriage Encounter, and Mary Rousseau's philosophy of human relationships. Like any good marriage, though, the book is not a 50-50 proposition, but a 100-100 exchange. With intimate couples, there is no longer anything that is "his" or "hers." Everything is theirs. So with our book. None of it is Chuck's alone, none of it Mary's. We did, it is true, begin with our own ideas and experiences, even as every marriage begins with two separate individuals. But during the two years that we spent in writing the book, we had so many conversations, so many exchanges of tapes and typescripts, that ideas and experiences which originally belonged to one or the other of us now truly belong to both.

Both of us, then, are equal in authorship. When Mary's experiences are reported in the first person (as in, "One day my son asked . . ."), the

1

use of "I" and "My" is purely for stylistic reasons. Chuck's experiences are reported in the third person for the same reason (as in "Chuck has learned from his couples. . ."). We are both agreed on every point that is included in the book. But one of us had to do the final writing. It is very difficult even for the most agreeable partners to work at a typewriter together, and that is why "I" means Mary, while "he" refers to Chuck.

Our main theme is that the passion of sexual intimacy builds the Church by continually widening the circle of those who love each other. It is our fondest hope that this product of our professional intimacy, in which philosophy and pastoral experience are wedded, may also have that same effect among couples and those whose lives they touch.

Mary Rousseau
Chuck Gallagher

Introduction

> I think God is calling you to something very special. I think He wants you to go with Him all the way. And I think you will be sorry if you don't do that.

The person speaking was a nun whom I admired and respected. She was telling me that she thought I had a religious vocation, specifically a call to join her order. Her advice wasn't new to me. I had heard similar remarks from priests and teachers throughout my high school and college years. And these people meant well. But the advice bothered me a great deal. Why did "going with God all the way" mean religious life? I certainly wanted to be wholehearted and generous with God, to love Him with my whole heart and soul, mind and strength. And yet, I also wanted very much to be married and have a family. Yet, the message I kept getting was that being married was somehow less than "going with God". A way of life defined by the Church as a sacrament was seen as a holding back, and to me — at least in my adolescent enthusiasm — holding back meant being selfish and ungrateful, perhaps even risking hell.

It was many years — more than I care to tell — before I worked my way out of my confusion. I suspect that such confusion was rather common to many other people, too, and probably still is. Marriage is often seen as a distraction to the love of God. Attention to spouse and family seems, to many people, to take attention away from God. Sexual passion is thought of as a distraction from prayer. In other words, married people are inferior Christians. Those who really wish to live the Christian ideal, to accept God's grace and do His will with generous hearts, are monks, priests, and nuns. Married people are second-class citizens in the Church. After all, how many canonized married saints are there? Can you think of even one couple who have been canonized as a couple, held up as models of holiness achieved through sexual passion? A few years ago there was some public talk of making Jacques and Raissa

Maritain the first such canonized couple. But even there — the Maritains had a celibate marriage. Something still keeps us from affirming the holiness of sex.

In a way, this situation is a tribute to monastic spirituality which has developed wonderfully over the centuries. Religious orders have given us many saints to admire and imitate. There is no doubt in anyone's mind that a life of poverty, chastity and obedience, a life of intense and prolonged daily prayer and regular spiritual direction can lead people to holiness. But the other side of that coin has been somewhat neglected. Instead of developing another spirituality, one that is appropriate for couples and families, we have encouraged those couples who want to be holy to imitate religious life as much as they can. Holy couples, then, are those who go to Church often, who do spiritual reading, who have regular prayer rituals and other pious practices in their homes. We don't really have a vision of Christian life that is special to married life, which has sexual intimacy as its main feature.

What, basically, is special to married life? This question is not so easy to answer. Many people say, "Well, a couple goes through a wedding ceremony, and that is a sacrament. But after that, their religious life is much the same as anyone's else's — mass, other prayers, social action, confession, reading religious books." There is a bit of truth in this view, for the fundamentals of holiness and a spiritual life are the same for everyone, married or not. We have the same commandments, the same ecclesiastical rituals, whether married or not. But mostly this attitude is wrong. It is not opposite to the truth, but it is a partial and seriously inadequate view. It misses some of the basic elements of all of Christian life. And it misses almost completely what is special to married life. For the sacrament of matrimony is not the wedding ceremony. It is something deeper and longer-lasting. It is sexual intimacy, day in and day out, throughout the life of a couple.

Before we can understand this sacrament, we need to rethink the basics of Christian life and spirituality. Briefly, the spiritual life of anyone who wishes to be saved is a life of intimacy with the Three Divine Persons. The inner life of God, of those three persons, is an intimacy, too — a totally perfect, divine intimacy. And so we might say that life for all Christians is one of intimacy with each other, and in and through that intimacy, a life of intimacy with Father, Son and Spirit. That is what Jesus came to bring us, life eternal. He promised that, if we would keep His commandments, He and His Father would come to live in us. So we are to live in God, and allow God to live in us. And the chief commandment we have to keep is the commandment to love — to love God with our whole hearts, our whole souls, with all our minds, and all our strength, and to love our neighbor as ourselves. Love creates a bond between people, and between people and God. And that bond is what we mean by intimacy, intimacy with Intimacy.

The English word *intimacy* comes from a Latin word meaning "within," or "inside". It's hard to picture how one person can live inside another. It certainly does not happen in a physical way. When a cannibal eats a missionary, for example, there is no intimacy. The missionary isn't "in" the cannibal — he has been assimilated into the cannibal, but he doesn't exist there as the person that he was before he was eaten. The presence of one person inside another is a psychological presence. When people are intimate with each other, they have a close kind of communion, a presence within each other, that leaves them physically intact in their original identities. Such communion seems strange when we try to understand it. But we know that it happens. We know from our experience what it is to have someone on our minds, or to carry someone in our hearts. It means having someone present in our thoughts and affections, our memories and hopes.

Such intimacy, the psychological presence of one person "in" another, is found most perfectly in God. God is not a single person, an individual in cool detachment from other persons. God is three persons in the deepest possible communion with each other. They have quite separate identities. The Father is Father, not Son or Spirit. The Son's identity is His alone, He is never Father or Spirit. And the Spirit's Self is unique, too. These Persons are more distinct from each other than we can begin to understand or imagine. They don't merge or blend into a single personality. And yet, they are so intimate to each other, so present within each other, that they are only one God — not three. In their knowing and loving of each other, they hold nothing back for themselves. The Father abandons His entire Self to his Son and Spirit, and Son and Spirit do the same. The love that circulates among them is so perfect that their communion with each other is perfect, too.

That is the kind of God we believe in. We cannot understand such unity among such distinctive persons. But that is the mystery we believe, the mystery of the Trinity. We may try to separate one person from the other in our minds, but that is a mistake. For example, we call ourselves Christians, followers of Christ, as if Jesus Christ could be Who He is all by Himself, without Father and Son. Actually, we should call ourselves "Trinitarians." We belong to the First Trinitarian Church. Jesus is not, all by Himself, the center of our spiritual life. Our *spiritual* life is just that — our life in and with the Spirit, the Spirit of Jesus. Jesus sends us that Spirit. And He is sent by His Father — sent to do His Father's will, to bring us His Father's words. He loves us because we are His Father's chosen ones. The Trinity, all three Persons together, is the core of all of our spirituality. Father, Son, and Spirit in their Intimacy with each other should be the center of our life in the Church. The Trinity should constantly affect the way that we think of ourselves. All of our prayer, all of our piety, all of our life should be centered on the Three Persons in One God.

The Trinity, then, is not just a dry dogma in the theology books. When we pray to the Son, we should be highly conscious of His Father and Spirit. And yet, we should not pray to all three in exactly the same way. Our decisions, our morality, our piety, and our daily interactions with each other should somehow be distinctively marked by the belief that God is Three. The Intimacy of the Trinity should be the center of our lives. If we are honest, though, we must admit that we tend to do one of two things, both of which leave the Trinity out of the picture. We either pray to some vague, undifferentiated "God", thinking of no Person in particular. Or else we think of them as three separate persons, praying to one in isolation from the others. I used to pray to one person — Jesus, for example, and then tell myself, "Oops! I'd better say a few words to Father and Spirit before I go, so they won't feel left out." There was a lot of confusion in that prayer, but at least I wasn't praying to some vague "God" who was no person in particular.

Jesus made a strong link between divine intimacy (the intimacy within the Trinity) and human intimacy (our intimacy with each other) at the Last Supper. He said that, if we keep His commandments, He and His Father would come to live in us (and persons living in each other is intimacy). At the Last Supper, though, He showed us, in action, what it means to keep His commandments. In fact, He gave a new commandment — that we love each other as he had loved us. And then He showed us, in the symbolic act of washing the feet of the disciples, what such love really means. It means intimacy. Remember how Peter protested? "Lord, you will never wash my feet." "Unless I do," Jesus said, "you shall have no heritage with me." And then Peter wanted to be washed all over! The usual interpretation of the foot-washing is that it was an act of humility, in which Jesus stooped as a servant to meet a humble physical need. What His action meant for us, then, was that we should serve each other, care for each other's needs.

But another interpretation is possible. In Jesus' time, washing someone's feet was an important Jewish symbol of hospitality. It was very practical, of course. When people walked through fields or on dirt roads in sandals, their feet got dirty and needed to be washed. But when the Jews washed the feet of their guests, they meant that action as an invitation to enter the intimacy of the family home. They wanted their guests to be physically comfortable, of course (and they also wanted to keep their own houses as clean as possible). But washing someone's feet did not mean, "Well, O.K., you can come in. But don't get the floor dirty. And don't take part in the life and conversation of the family. Sit quietly in the corner." No, the Jews who washed their guests' feet were inviting them to take full part in the life that went on in their homes. And that life was not just a life of human intimacy. It was their religious life. So the Jewish host said to his guests, "Welcome. Please join us in our intimacy with our God, the Bridegroom of Israel." Later on, the Benedictine monks took up this traditional Jewish gesture of hospitality. They washed the feet of their guests as a symbolic way of welcoming them into the intimate life of the monastery. That life was their intimacy with Christ, the Bridegroom of the Church, and with His Father and Spirit.

When Jesus finished washing the feet of His disciples, He prayed His great prayer for intimacy—intimacy among His followers, and between His Father and Spirit.

> Father, that they may all be one; even as thou, Father, art in me, and I in thee, that they also may be one in us, so that the world may believe that thou hast sent me. (Jn 17:21)

But Trinitarian intimacy is not the only basic feature of our life in the Church. Our life is also sacramental. We are the only Church in the world that believes in seven sacraments, seven human actions that are, in some special way, symbolic causes of the communion of human intimates with the Intimacy of God. Such actions as Baptism, Matrimony, and Eucharist are symbols of divine life. But they are not *just* symbols. They cause the life that they signify. They have a healing, redeeming effect on us. And that healing effect is, precisely, our communion with each other and with God. One way of looking at the sacraments, then, at the sacramental way of life that is special to us Trinitarians, is to see them as healing, or reversing, the effects of the sin of Adam.

Scripture scholars tell us not to read the Adam and Eve story literally, as if the Fall was an event that occurred in history. Rather, the story is a myth, a symbolic explanation of certain constant features of the human condition that are hard to understand. One fact that all of us human beings experience is that we fear intimacy and try to avoid it. The tendency to avoid intimacy is the shame that Adam and Eve felt after eating the forbidden fruit. They hid themselves, from each other and from God. Their shame was not just an embarrassment at being naked—a feeling all of us know well. It was much deeper, something like what psychologists call self-contempt. It is a deep sense of being unworthy and unlovable as persons. When we have such a negative attitude toward ourselves, we tend to shy away from other people, to avoid getting too close to them. We do not let other people take us into their minds and hearts in loving familiarity. Instead, we stay aloof and protect ourselves. We keep our distance, hiding our very persons as well as our physical nakedness. The sacramental life of the Church is meant to heal that shame, to give us the realization that we are loved, and are lovable, so that we can open up to each other in true intimacy. And as we do that, we come into intimacy with God—Father, Son, and Spirit. Sacraments, then, both symbolize and cause the divine life in us. They enable us to love as Jesus did, so that He, His Father, and His Spirit come to live in us.

Marriage, though, is special. It holds a unique place in our set of sacraments. For matrimony symbolizes, and causes, the divine life in us in a way that no other sacrament can do. In the sexual intimacy of sacramental couples, we have a model of the intimacy that all human beings are called to that is more clear, more dramatic, and easier to understand, than any other model we can name. Over the centuries, celibate life has been held up as the ideal and model for everyone to follow, so that married people were to imitate monastic life as best they could in their families. But actually, it should be the other way around. Married life, the sexual intimacy of couples, should be held up as the model for celibates. Celibate holiness is, in one way, the higher kind—closer to what Jesus lived, and closer to what all of us will be in heaven. But even celibate life is a kind of sexual intimacy. And marriage is a revelation of sexual intimacy that is easier for the average person to recognize and understand. Perhaps that is the reason why the great majority of the world's people have sought their salvation in marriage rather than in religious life.

It is surprising to think that married life is a model for celibates, rather than the other way around! We won't be surprised, though, if we can get a clear grasp of some important ideas about the life of Trinitarian intimacy—the life to which all of Jesus' followers are called. First of all, we need to realize that we are all celibates. Some of us are celibates to everyone we meet—those of us who are not married. But those of us who are married are also celibates—to everyone in the world except our spouses. And that celibacy is very important. For all of us are called to love, to love our neighbor as ourselves. And we are called to love with our whole selves, our feelings as well as our wills, our bodies as well as our souls. Any whole and healthy love, then, any love given by any one person to any other person, is going to be sexual love in some sense. The only way in which we could conceive of love as not being sexual would be to think of it as the love of a pure spirit. Angels can love without feelings, without sexual passion. But human beings cannot. When we try to eliminate or repress our sexual feelings, we inhibit our love. And inhibited love is not the kind that brings about our intimacy with God.

Let's make that idea more concrete. I, as a married woman, love my husband, and love him sexually. I try to give my whole self to him, and accept his gift of his whole self to me. We love each other not just with our minds and wills, but with feelings and bodies — sexual feelings, sexed bodies. That much is easy. But — and here is the amazing thing — as a follower of Jesus, I am to love my neighbor as myself. And every other human being in the world, past, present, and future, is my neighbor. If all love is to be humanly whole, it must be whole hearted. I must love all people with my feelings and my body. Now, my feelings and my body are sexual. I am a woman, and not a man, in every fiber of my being. There is no ounce or inch of me that is not marked by my sexuality. The conclusion, then, is clear: I am, as a follower of Jesus, expected to love everyone with a sexual love, to love everyone in an intimacy that is somehow sexual. Does being married mean I must love no other man than my husband? Of course not. I am to love everyone. Thus I must love many other men: my relatives and friends, my colleagues at work, those I am connected with in social and political life, and so on. And my love for these men is sexual. So is my love for women. All of human love is sexual, married or celibate, because all human beings, married or celibate, are sexual. Of course when we say *sexual* we don't necessarily mean sexual intercourse. We're referring to what Pope John Paul II calls "the nuptial meaning of the body". Everyone's body has a nuptial meaning, because God created us male and female, and then "saw that it was very good". But what is that nuptial meaning? First of all, it is a kind of incompleteness. No man or woman alone has all that it takes to produce a child. But that incompleteness exists on other levels, too. No man or woman alone has all that it takes to be a person. All of us, in order to be whole, have to have some kind of loving communion with people of the opposite sex. It is not just our germ cells that are incomplete without the other sex — our personalities are, too. Every cell of our bodies is marked by our sexuality. A trained biologist can look at any cell of a human body, and tell whether it came from a man or a woman. And if and when psychologists perfect their techniques, they will be able to tell how men and women perceive reality differently, and differ in feelings and emotions.

The English word *sex* may derive from the Latin term that means "to cut off, or separate." But sex doesn't just mean incompleteness or separation from those who have what we lack. Sex also means complementarity. In germ cells and sexual organs, men and women complement, complete, fill each other wonderfully. And the same complementarity shows up in our personal selves, too. Women need men's perceptions and feelings in order to be psychologically whole and complete. And men need women's. We all need some sort of communion, intimacy, with people of the opposite sex. Since marriage is the clearest example we have of intersexual intimacy, of men and women sharing life with each other in a rather complete way, everybody's need for some such intimacy is aptly called nuptial. It is because we are sexed beings — not asexual, and not hermaphrodites — that we need intimacy in order to be complete persons. Celibates need that as much as anyone else. Spouses need it with other people as well as with each other. That need for intersexual intimacy is the nuptial meaning of our human bodies.

It makes sense, then, for matrimony to be a sacrament — a symbolic cause, and causal symbol — of intimacy. For marriage spells total and permanent belonging between persons in a way that no other human state or action can do. When a man is only living with a woman, for example, he cannot very easily miss a day's work in order to take care of her when she's sick. "It's not as if you're married, you know." But all employers allow people to miss work to take care of a sick spouse. There is a special belonging, a special unity between spouses that does not happen between other pairs and groups of people. Likewise, when we are permanently committed to something — to a job, say, or a house — we speak of being wedded or married to it. "I could move tomorrow," we might say. "I'm not wedded to Milwaukee, after all." Or, "You'll never get him to change jobs — he's married to that company." Marriage means a unity that is permanent and complete. But the love that all followers of Jesus have for each other is also permanent and complete. All love, all unity, all intimacy should resemble a marriage. It should be as total and as permanent as circumstances allow. That is why marriage is the model for celibate love rather than celibate love being the model for marriage.

'The nuptial meaning of the body,' then, is just a new phrase that refers to one of the Church's constant traditions. Our redemptive, spiritual life is communal, not individualistic. We believers in the Trinity cannot live as private individuals with some sort of vertical, one-to-one relationship with God. We are saved in and through our intimacy with each other, and in no other way. And our intimacy joins us to the Trinitarian intimacy that is the interior life of God. God is no solitary individual, but a Trinity of Persons, Father, Son and Spirit, joined in eternal intimacy, in a love that is total and permanent. And so, nuptial intimacy — whether between spouses, among celibates, or between celibates and married folk — mirrors the inner life of God and actually takes part in it.

> The Church could stop teaching the Trinity tomorrow, and begin preaching an individual God, and it wouldn't make one iota of difference to the daily lives of most of her members.

The great German Jesuit theologian, Karl Rahner, made a remark similar to that recently. And isn't it true that the Church could stop teaching Matrimony — the sacrament — tomorrow and that it wouldn't make much difference, either? People would still get married, of course, and still pray and worship pretty much as they do now. Who ever thinks of the Trinity as a model for how we should live? Who ever prays to the Three Divine Persons as intimate friends? And who ever thinks of married life as an entry into the life that those three persons share with each other? Matrimony and the Trinity have not been widely appreciated, nor widely preached. And the spiritual life is often presented to us — and accepted by us — in moralistic terms. We try to live for our own individual moral perfection rather than for intimacy. We tend to think that living a good life means doing right actions, rather than relating to others in intimacy.

What is even worse, all too often our moralism is duty-oriented. Even when we do value human relationships, we think that these are built by doing good actions to and for each other. Morally good actions are those in which we act deliberately, freely recognizing some duty and dutifully obeying the rules. A good person is a morally upright one, someone who adheres to principles and lives up to obligations. I saw this moralism very graphically one day when a little girl got sick and began vomiting at the children's mass. I took her to the bathroom, helped her as best I could, then sought one of the sisters in charge. She took one look at the situation, patted me on the shoulder and said, "My dear, you've done your work of supererogation for the day." She was perfectly serious. Now, there is moralism in all its splendor. We organize our days around meeting our obligations and fulfilling our duties. And anything beyond that is a work of supererogation. Intimacy and love don't even enter the picture.

But what about the little girl? The sister did not even acknowledge her presence or speak to her. She spoke about her, in the third person, as if she wasn't even there. Later, as I walked the girl to her home, I found out that her father had died recently, and her younger brother was home with the measles. Here was a sad and frightened little person who needed someone's spontaneous sympathy and concern. In fact, studies have shown that children who lose a parent by death need most of all to have some other adult who will be crazy about them, and let it show. They don't need to be someone's work of supererogation for the day. They need someone to love them forever, with warmth and enthusiasm, simply for being the person they are. And that is what all of us need from each other — someone to be crazy about us, to love us spontaneously for being who we are, to show an enthusiasm that is total and long lasting. That need, and our ability to meet that need for each other, is the nuptial meaning of our bodies. And its clearest model is the sexual intimacy of couples.

But we don't just abuse and misuse each other when we live life as a series of actions in which we dutifully obey rules and commandments. We actually construct and worship an idol, a false God. God has revealed Himself as a Lover, not a Rule-Giver. He is an Intimacy of persons united with each other in perfect understanding and love, and He invites us into that intimacy. Moral principles, laws and rules are important, of course. We are not recommending a thoughtless enthusiasm and im- pulsive behavior. We need a devotion to duty that is, at least sometimes, heroic. We need a fidelity to principles that often goes against the grain. But obedience to duty is a means to an end, not an ideal. It is a fall- back position for those times when we are not our best selves. Even then, we have to be careful not to make God into some sort of masochist. We mustn't think of Him as a stern taskmaster who requires difficult things of us and threatens us with punishment if we fail. Sometimes we think, in the back of our minds, that difficulty is what makes something right. We may even think that the harder something is, the better it is. But when we do that, we construct an idol. If we think that what counts the most with God is what costs us the most, we worship a false God, one that doesn't exist. What truly counts the most with God is what draws us most joyously into His inner life of love. What counts the most is our joyous intimacy with each other.

In his book on child-care, Dr. Spock remarks that each time a new baby learns to do something new — to sit up, to crawl, to walk, to talk — that discovery is just as new to the baby as it was to the very first human being who walked or talked for the first time in human history. One of the joys of raising children is watching each one repeat the whole history of the human race, learning all of those new things. In our spiritual lives, we need to do something similar, something that is even more exciting. Each of us has to repeat the entire history of the Church, as over the centuries she has come slowly to clarify her main teachings. Take the Incarnation, for example. We all say the Creed, and would not deny that Jesus Christ is both God and man. But we find it difficult to really live that belief, to fit flesh and spirit together in a way that makes sense. In fact, we find it hard to get flesh and spirit together in our understanding of ourselves. It is much easier to keep these in separate compartments. What we do physically, then, which includes our emotional life and our sexual activity, is kept separate from our religious beliefs and practices. It is, indeed, a rare Catholic who succeeds in getting his prayer and his sexuality completely together.

The confusion is even deeper when we look at our concept of Jesus, where we must integrate not just flesh and spirit, but divine life and human life. Jesus is not just an enfleshed soul, but an enfleshed God. We easily picture Him in the back of our minds as someone who came with a mission to do certain deeds and propose certain teachings, to give us an example of how we should live. And His supreme example, of course, was in His death on the cross. That, we think, was a martyrdom. Jesus did what was hard, and merited our salvation by the awful pain He felt. But what was most important about Jesus was not His deeds and His teachings, nor the pain of crucifixion: it was that He lived in intimacy with His Father and Spirit, and that He did not depart from that intimacy in His Incarnation. He came, rather, to draw us into that intimacy, too — in and through our intimacy with each other; His deeds, His teachings, His crucifixion were all means to that. What was important about His death was not the pain and suffering: His death was His entry into a new depth of intimacy with His Father and His Spirit, and His sending of that Spirit into us. That was its main point; death led to Resurrection, to Ascension, to sending His Spirit.

Does this seem like a fine point, one for theologians to quibble about? It is not. It is the difference between the kind of love in which we are supposed to spend our lives and an unhealthy masochism. Jesus is the Bridegroom of the Church. But like other bridegrooms, He does not love his bride out of a patronizing and controlling superiority. He loves us because He sees in us a goodness that He finds irresistibly attractive. Isn't that how any bridegroom loves His bride? And the goodness that Jesus sees in us, and is drawn to, is our status as His Father's chosen, beloved people. He sees His Father's mark on us, and is drawn by an irresistible desire to make us His intimates. His love for us is not a stiff-upper lipped endurance, but a heartfelt longing to become one flesh with us, to make us members of His own body. Ask any bridegroom how close he would like to be with his bride. That desire is a reflection — a pale reflection, but a real one — of Jesus's love for us.

The Bible speaks often in metaphors of married life. Yahweh is the Bridegroom, Israel His cherished bride, even in her infidelity. Jesus is the Bridegroom of the Church. God is the Bridegroom of all of creation. These metaphors are no accident. They speak to people in words that are easy to understand and are full of power. The best antidote, then, to our deep tendency to moralize, to act out of duty, to see God and Jesus as stern task-masters, is a better understanding of the sacrament of matrimony. The best way to get rid of idols is to smash them with a blunt instrument. The most powerful instrument we know for crushing a moralistic approach to life is sex. It is the sacrament of matrimony. With a better appreciation of that sacrament, we would begin to worship the true God, the one God in three divine persons who invites us to intimacy with Himself. We would fulfill Jesus' new command, enacted in the foot-washing, that we love each other as He has loved us. We would begin to enjoy the nuptial meaning of our bodies. And then, wouldn't we be noticed? By the love that we would then have for each other, all men would know that we are the disciples of Jesus. We would be, ourselves, sacraments.

Fortunately, we are not always logical or honest enough to really live out what we have in the back of our minds as ideals and principles. For example, what is it we wish for our children and friends at their weddings? What did we marrieds wish for ourselves at *our* weddings? It wasn't a grim set of duties and responsibilities which, if they were difficult enough, might win us our salvation when we die. We don't wish that newlyweds will find ways to keep a certain distance from each other, working out their fulfillment as independent, dutiful individuals. We don't hope to see them doing good deeds for each other. And we certainly do not wish their home life to be a constant round of "churchy" activities — prayers, rituals, pious practices, Bible readings. Please God, religious rituals will have a place in all of our homes. But it will not be an artificial imitation of what goes on in Church.

To put it simply, we wish happiness for newlyweds as we did for ourselves. We want the simple happiness and joy that come with intimacy. We want spouses to like each other, to enjoy each other, to live in a constant warmth of desire for each other. We wish them the continuing joy of the passion that they already feel in their peak moments of sexual desire. In that passion, if we stop and look at it, we can see all the elements of a Catholic spirituality of marriage. For passion is interpersonal, not individualistic. It is spontaneous and intimate, not abstract and dutiful. It makes moral goodness a joy, not a grim and difficult task. And it is deeply incarnational, bringing our whole selves, and even the entire physical world, into the love that joins us to God. Finally, passion is Trinitarian. It is our best imitation of, and participation in, the intimacy enjoyed by Father, Son, and Spirit. And so, it is to the unleashing of passion that we now turn.

CHAPTER ONE

Sex Is Sacramental

> Your basic problem is that you are deeply and thoroughly self-centered, and you aren't even aware of it. So, you need to do two things. First, pray for an awareness of the fact. And then pray for the courage to do something about it. Because it will mean changing your whole way of life.

The words were blunt, but I had asked for it. I had been going to confession routinely every week or two, and not making much progress in becoming a better person. And I had asked my confessor why. He spoke these words and then walked away, leaving me alone with my thoughts and with my God. It was the painful beginning of a new life. The beginning is not yet over—just when I think it is, it happens all over again. But that confession did bring an insight that has held for more than twenty years: that our baptism as Catholics gives us a new identity. Life in the Church is a call to leave behind our isolated, individual selves, and our concern for them, our centering on them. In leaving our self-centeredness behind, we come into our new identity: our intimacy with Father, Son and Spirit, in and through our intimacy with each other.

A couple of enthusiastic young street missionaries stopped me one day and offered me some religious literature. I politely said, "No, thank you." Then one of them asked me, "But do you know whether or not you are saved?" I said, "Yes, I am." "Have you accepted Jesus Christ as your personal Savior?" "Yes, I have." Then, with a big smile, the young man said, "Really?" I said, "Yes, really. I am a Roman Catholic." At that, the smile disappeared and the two walked on down the street, looking slightly stunned, not knowing what to say next. Catholics are not expected to have a personal relationship with Jesus. People tend to see us as loyal to a big, impersonal organization, and obedient to its rules.

Well, we do, of course, belong to the institutional Church, with her hierarchy, her teaching and moral authority, her rules and regulations. But all of that is secondary. What really makes us belong to the Church is our intimacy with Jesus, His Father and His Spirit, in and through our intimacy with each other. Our life in the Church is not primarily moral, but sacramental. And sacraments both cause and symbolize intimacy.

Jesus prayed for that intimacy at the Last Supper, shortly after He commanded us to love: "Father, may they be one in us, as you are in me and I am in you, so that the world may believe it was you who sent me." (Jn 17:21). There is our life in the Church in a nutshell. It is awesome when we stop to think about it. We are to be sacraments — not just receive sacraments, or dispense them, or perform them — we are, ourselves, to be sacraments to the world. The new identities that we take on at our baptisms are meant to show the world that Jesus was sent by His Father. And the way we show that is by actually being in the divine persons, just as they are in each other. How in the world can one person be "in" another? There is only one way — through love. Love is the tie that binds people together. It is the core of Jesus' longing for us, His way of being our personal savior, the mission that he gives us all. He wants us to live in a loving intimacy with each other that will make His unity with His Father credible to the rest of the world.

Well, we can see our readers cringe at the word *love*. Is there any other word in the English language that is more over-used? Is there any other word that has so many confused, and confusing, meanings? Is there any other reality in human life that is more elusive? And yet, we have no other choice. "God is Love. And he who lives in love lives in God, and God in Him." (I John 4:21) Those simple words tell how the intimacy that saves us is formed. We aren't just born intimates, after all. Intimacy is something we have to build, and love is the way to do that. But first we have to understand love. Obviously the love that is sacramental is not the love we might have for pizza, or a favorite dress. Nor is it the dreamy, sentimental romance described in cheap novels. Neither is it the vulgar, casual sex that pervades our culture. *The Love Boat* and *Three's Company*, two of our most popular TV programs, call that kind of sex *love*. But it is neither the kind of love we have in mind, nor the kind of sex.

The dictionary definition is not a bad place to start. Love, says Webster, is "a tender, passionate affection for one of the opposite sex." The term has other meanings, of course, but this is the first one. It describes quite well what we mean by love, what we refer to as *sex*, throughout this book. The definition has several elements, all of them important. The first one may seem too obvious to mention: affection. Affection is a benevolent feeling toward someone. It means wishing that person well, wanting good things for him or her. We often hear that, as Christians, we have to love everybody, but we don't have to like them. That statement is not very realistic. True, we can find people repulsive, not to our liking, and still wish them well and do good things for them. But such well-wishing will not go very deep or last very long unless our feelings become involved, too. We can't have any significant intimacy with someone we don't like. That is especially true in marriage. A marriage in which the spouses don't really like each other—and there are a lot of such marriages—will not be sacramental, not a luminous revelation of the God who is Love.

Tenderness and passion, the other two elements of the definition of love, almost seem contradictory. To many people's minds, sexual passion is rough and violent, a selfish, brute force. Sometimes children are frightened when they see men and women making love; they think they are fighting. But passion and violence don't have to go together. Passion and vigorous, energetic activity—yes, but passionate people can also be tender, kind, gentle, loving. Passion can be a lusty affection. Jeremiah tells us to circumcize the foreskins of our hearts. To married people, this has to mean making passion tender and tenderness passionate. One without the other is simply not sacramental.

The sacrament of matrimony is heat and energy that carry tender affection. All followers of Jesus have to have a kind of heart transplant. We have to let God take away our hearts of stone and give us hearts of flesh. Now, what is the difference between these two kinds of hearts? For couples, the difference is passion. Sexual desire operates on hearts that are cold, hard, insensitive, and lifeless, and makes them warm, soft, sensitive, and pulsating with life. Passion truly tenderizes people. And tenderized people are sacramental. They show everybody that God is Love, and that he who lives in love lives in God, and God in Him. They make love attractive, and draw other people to live in it. They make God attractive and draw other people to live in Him. And that is exactly how a sacrament works.

Robert Louis Stevenson noticed that process. He said:

> Love makes people believe in immortality, because there seems not to be room enough in life for so great a tenderness, and it is inconceivable that the most masterful of our emotions should have no more than the spare moments of a few brief years.

All of our sacraments are meant to show love to people in a way that will make them believe in immortality. Let's think about the experiences which reassure us about our religious beliefs. Don't we all have moments when we say, in a flash of realization, "My gosh, yes—it really is true! God, life after death—everything." As often as not, those flashes of realization come when we are in contact with people whom we find especially attractive and credible. But all such people have one important quality in common—they easily give and receive love. They are obviously convinced that life is good. They find life happy, meaningful, well worth living. And that is because they believe in the reality of human love. When we meet such people, we are drawn to them. We like to be with them. We want to be like them, to enjoy life as they do. They are sacraments.

When a couple, through their passion, become sacramental to others, their love becomes what Stevenson calls it—a great tenderness. Loving, passionate couples feel an enormous, almost overwhelming concern for every single human being. They are aware of the goodness of people, a goodness so poignant that they could contemplate it all day long. They feel the pain of every human indignity, every rejection of one person by another, every neglect or abuse of anyone anywhere. They cannot watch the evening news in calm complacency: "Oh, yeah, starving babies. But that's way off in Africa somewhere, no concern of mine." That kind of indifference is not possible for loving couples. Their passion so tenderizes their hearts that they feel everyone's suffering as their own.

This sounds strange, at first. Usually we think of a passionate couple as so absorbed in each other that they don't even notice what's going on around them. But love, especially sexual love, has great power to crack our shells and open us up to other people, to the whole world. As Stevenson says, it becomes the most masterful of our emotions. When spouses let their passion have its sway, they gradually find that love takes over their lives. Their anger and grief are ruled by love, rather than the other way around. Don't we all know people who seem to be angry at the world? They seem to take a critical and complaining attitude toward everyone. They even sound angry when they don't mean to be. Love can master such anger, tenderize hearts, make them flexible instead of brittle. On my sacramental days, for example—my passionate days—I discipline my children differently. Take, for example, a simple thing such as wiping up shower splashes from the bathroom floor. Children forget: They have their minds on other things. And so they need repeated reminders. But I find myself giving these reminders in two different ways. On my bad days, days when I have allowed my passion for Ed to cool and my tenderness to go to sleep, I will be irritated with the children: "Eddie, come here right now and wipe up this water. How many times have I told you not to do this? What's the matter with you, anyway? Don't you care? Don't you listen to me?" Such remarks hardly foster a child's belief in immortality because he is experiencing love as someone's most masterful emotion. But on my good days — my passionate loving, tender days — I hand out the needed correction in a much different way: "Honey, I know it's hard to remember these little things, and usually you do, but we do need to keep this floor dry all the time. Would you please try to remember next time? Thanks."

What is it like, then, for love to be the most masterful of our emotions? Think of all the different feelings we experience from time to time — not just anger and grief, but fear, despair, hope, joy, and courage. Love can master these. Love can come to be the master of our lives. In the words of the popular song, "Every breath you take, every vow you make, every step you take" can be done for love and in love, can come out of love and grow into it. When we first try to love in all things, it might seem difficult, contrived, against the grain. But later love becomes spontaneous and gracious, the easier way, a second nature. That is how our life in the Church is meant to change us all. We gradually take on new identities of lovers. And when that happens, we will use a wonderful phrase: when, from time to time, our tenderness fails, we will apologize and say, "Please forgive me — I wasn't myself when I said that."

When love is life — not just isolated moments here and there, but life, all day and all night — then it is indeed inconceivable that it should have any limits at all. We can see something very important in the way that people usually react to a broken romance. Don't they often become a little cynical, saying to themselves, "Aw, it was never real to begin with. I'll never fall for that trap again." Fortunately, most people get over that cynicism. But a few never do. Some remain suspicious of love all the rest of their lives. Now, that cynicism can tell us something. If love is real, it lasts forever. If it doesn't last, even when we want it to last with all our hearts, then it wasn't real. Deep down in our hearts we know that love has to have a permanent quality, that it has to be stronger than death. Since this is true, it is easy to go from believing in the reality of love to believing in immortality.

When love does get to be something that we are, rather than something that we feel from time to time, when it really is an atmosphere that we breathe in and breathe out, then it is, indeed, inconceivable that it should last but a few brief years. Once we become lovers, a whole lifetime is really not enough to do all the loving that we want to do. We can never have enough of love, and even after a long life — 80 years or so — it seems brief, indeed. The thought that death might be the end of loving, that death might be stronger than love, is outrageous, horrifying, intolerable! For this great tenderness cries out to last forever. And so, time pushes us into a corner. Eventually we have to make up our minds, once and for all: do we believe in immortality, or don't we? Do we believe that love is real, or don't we?

Last winter, I went to a very sad funeral. A friend of mine had died suddenly of a heart attack, at the age of 58. His family had all gathered for Christmas, and were sitting in their living room, talking, when Bill suddenly fell over, dead. At his funeral, his youngest son, John, age 22, began to sob uncontrollably. At that moment, his sister, who was sitting between John and their mother, very spontaneously and graciously got up and traded places with John. He put his head in his mother's lap and continued to sob, as her arms enfolded him. The gesture was a powerful revelation to me. It showed the kind of love that was so much a part of that family's life. They didn't need a whispered consultation about what to do. The daughter simply stood up, her brother moved over, his mother enfolded him in her arms. I could easily imagine literally hundreds of situations in the history of that family, in which brothers and sisters, and parents and children, husband and wife showed such spontaneous love for each other. At that funeral, I came to know Bill, and to feel his presence, more deeply, and more vividly than I had when he was alive.

Love, then, makes us believe in immortality. I knew Bill was still alive, and always will be, because of the love which his children had learned from him and his wife. But the decision to believe in love, in immortality, in the Trinity and our intimacy with God, is always a choice. We have to decide freely whether to believe in these realities or not. There is no scientific proof — no litmus paper or other scientific evidence — which can prove that anyone ever loves anyone, that love is ever real. But our decision to believe in love is not a blind leap in the dark, either. As C.S. Lewis once put it, it is not wishful thinking, but thoughtful wishing. Our religious beliefs come out of our experiences of people. If we know people in whom we can see passion, tenderness, and love, the choice becomes easy. We begin to believe in immortality because we believe that love is real, and real love has to last forever.

Stevenson's words, then, describe the sacramental power of love. Jesus mentioned this power, too, when He said just after the footwashing at the Last Supper: "By this will all men know that you are my disciples, that you love one another." Our love for each other can have a drawing power that will bring people into the Church and deepen the faith of those who are already in it. The Catholic Church is a missionary Church, with a desire to convert the entire human race. That mission tendency has gone astray at times, to be sure, when we have used the wrong

methods. A Jesuit philosopher I once knew boasted one day of having
an atheist in his parlor. "I fired syllogism after syllogism at his head,"
the priest bragged, "and at the end of an hour, his head sank." Well, yes.
We can imagine his head sinking. But can we imagine his asking to enter
the Church because his encounter with love as a masterful emotion had
made him believe in immortality? Hardly.

Still, it is true, we are a missionary Church. And that mission begins
and ends in the lives of our people, as love becomes, day in and day out,
our most masterful emotion. We must have other things, too. We need
theology and catechetics, and preaching and teaching. We need social
justice and institutions for practicing the spiritual and corporal works
of mercy. But these are all means to an end. The end is making love our
most masterful emotion. Only then is love sacramental, revealing the
presence of God in human intimacy, and making that presence real. And
in matrimony, love takes on a special sacramental character for it is joined
to sexual passion. Nothing in the world has greater power than sex to
make love credible and real. Nothing in the world has greater power than
sex to bring about so great a tenderness, and to make it real.

It may seem surprising that we link tenderness and passion. To many
people passion means lust, violence, destruction. Passion certainly can
be self-seeking of an especially strong kind, a search for pleasure that
lets nothing get in its way. Another element of this popular view is that
men are more passionate than women, and once their sexual feelings
are aroused they can no longer control themselves. One of my college
professors told the Women's Sodality once, in all seriousness, that if boys
become sexually aroused and have an erection, they then must go on
to ejaculate, or else go crazy. For people who accept this myth of uncontrollable male passion, it is easy to think of men as beasts, and to
think of marriage as mainly giving them a legitimate outlet for their
uncontrollable brutish lust. The people who believe this myth are not
all women, either. In a later chapter we will have more to say about the
true sexual needs of men. For now, let us just say that an outlet for uncontrollable animal lust is not one of their genuine needs.

Tenderness is a need, however. Actually, passion and tenderness are
not opposites, but go together for both men and women. The relation
between passion and tenderness is what we call, in mathematics, a direct
ratio. That is, as one grows, so does the other. And as one declines, so
does the other. This ratio is the core of the sacrament of matrimony.
Marriage is sacramental because passion makes people tender, and tenderness makes them passionate. Notice that we did not say that marriage
reflects the passion of men and the tenderness of women. Passion and

tenderness go together in both sexes. The more tender a woman is, the more passionate she will be. The more she wishes to love tenderly, the more passionate she will become. A husband who wishes to be more passionate will also be more tender. It may be that, because of certain false ideas in our culture (which we all have, because we drink them in with our mothers' milk), women's passion has been somewhat repressed and so we have to work at it. Men, on the other hand, have had to withhold their tenderness, and we need to correct that. But the final result will be the same: the more passionate someone is, the more tender he or she will be, and the more tender, the more passionate. A couple will be sacramental precisely to the degree that they develop the tender passion, and the passionate tenderness, that is special to married love and intimacy. Love is the basic sacrament. Sexual love is the sacramental symbol of matrimony.

"I wouldn't do that for anyone else in the world. I might die for someone else — but I wouldn't do that. That is special, and especially for you, because you are so special." Gertrude was half-joking, as she and her husband basked in the afterglow of making love. He knew, after 25 years of happy, faithful married life, that her interest in anyone else as a sexual partner was simply unthinkable. And she knew that he knew. It was one of those topics that they didn't have to discuss. But she also knew that he liked to hear those words, and he knew that she knew. And so she made a fumbling and inadequate attempt to put into words what her actions had already said.

But those words, like the sexual act itself, capture the paradox of married love. The totality of it is a mysterious and wonderful thing. For in a way, all of us followers of Jesus, all of us Trinitarians, are called to love each other totally. We are commanded to love our neighbor as ourselves, to give up our lives for our friends. If I see a strange child toddle into traffic, for example, I cannot just watch and say, "Gee, isn't that too bad? I'm glad it's not one of my children." Jesus wants me to love all children, and all grownups, too. And so, I would try to save the child's life, even if I lost my own in the process. My love for everyone has to be that total. And yet, the totality of married love, expressed so clearly in the act of sexual intercourse, is special. As Gertrude said, she wouldn't do that for anyone else. She had seen how sex is sacramental. Intercourse, and the whole intimacy of married life, is an especially clear revelation of the totality of love. And such total love is what makes people believe in immortality.

Sex does not just reveal love, however. It has a special power to make love real, to bring people to the total commitment and gift of self to each other that it symbolizes. The power of sexual passion is proverbial. It is one of the strongest forces in human life. It can be, of course, a powerful evil force at times. If we read the newspapers and watch TV, we soon see that sex motivates many, if not most, of the murders that happen. But the sacramental power of sex is just as strong. In a later chapter, we will describe that energy more fully. People often think that the Church has paid too much attention to sex. Certainly, she has had a lot to say about it over the centuries. But some of the right things have not yet been said. Much of the message has been negative moralizing. What we need to do is to proclaim and celebrate the good news that sex is holy, sex is sacramental, sex is what builds the Church. It is the way to salvation for most people, the way to victory over sin and death. It is the path to love which, once it becomes our most masterful emotion, makes people believe in immortality.

I used to wonder a lot about what God does all day. Even if you believe that God is Three Persons, there is a problem about forming a concrete picture of that in your imagination. I used to think, for example, about heaven being an endless state of contemplation, in which we "see God face to face." Except that God doesn't have a face, really. So heaven would be an endless contemplation of pure spirit—or of three pure spirits. It didn't seem too exciting. And when I'd hear that our life of grace is a participation in the very life of God, I had to wonder what God's life is like. It's not like anything material, since God is pure spirit. And that seems pretty boring. I even thought it must be boring to God. What, after all, do Father, Son and Spirit do all day? Look at each other with blank stares? And then a friend of mine—a deeply spiritual man, a husband, father, and professor, and one of the most credible people I've ever met—one day used the phrase "the love play of the Trinity." Wow! Love play! Now there was something I could relate to! And so could anyone else who had experienced it. At that moment, sex became a sacrament for me, in an entirely new way. It spoke to me clearly and powerfully about what God is. But more, it made the presence of God real in my life as it had never been before.

And so in love play we can get some glimpse of what God does all day. The three divine persons, Father, Son and Spirit, play—play in love. Our moments of play are the high points of our days, are they not? We play when our work is done, when there are no more needs to be met, no services to be performed, no tasks or duties to be done—at least for a while. And so we simply relax and enjoy each other, enjoy the good that we see in each other, enjoy the life that we share with each other. And sexual ecstasy is a high point of play—more intense and vivid than any other kind. In our best sexual moments, all cares fall away, we gasp in realization of the person before us, we shriek in ecstasy at the realization that we two, wonderful as we are, belong to each other. That sexual moment, that moment of love play, deserves to be counted as one of our seven sacraments. It is most fitting, "truly right and just," that sexual intimacy should be a symbol — a causal symbol — of our intimacy with the three divine persons. Human love play is one clear and powerful way for human beings to take part in the love play of the Trinity.

But symbols have to be accurate. They have to really resemble what they symbolize,or else people will misinterpret them. An arrow on a highway sign that points in the wrong direction does not guide people to where they want to go. With sacraments, accuracy is especially important, for sacraments don't just point the way to something. They effectively cause it, make it real, in and through their symbolism. And since sacraments are human actions, they can go wrong. When they do, it is worse than an incorrect highway sign. A failed sacrament can be a defect in someone's eternal salvation.

We must be careful, then, that the love-making and the entire way of life of a couple says what it is meant to say. Couples, in order to be sacramental, must do much more than say their vows correctly at their wedding. They must live a whole life that says, loud and clear for all to hear, *love, intimacy, sex.* As the poet E. E. Cummings once put it,

> be of love (a little)
> more careful
> than of everything

Cummings deliberately left out all punctuation marks so that his poems could be read in several ways and thus have more than one meaning. Surely we can see in the verse above that we must be careful of love. Love doesn't just happen. It takes effort, care, nurture. Even a little bit of love is worthy of nurture. It is the most precious thing in the world. When we believe that sex is a sacrament, we can paraphrase a bit; we should be of sex (a little) more careful than of everything, too. Part of such care is in understanding better just what sex is, how it both symbolizes and causes ecstasy. We will take up that topic later. But for now, let's look at love once again, to see more deeply how it brings about intimacy.

Being born is a big shock to a new baby's system. It creates a huge separation between mother and child. It takes a baby many months to realize that he is no longer part of his mother, but a separate individual.

Nevertheless, the fact is there. Once we are expelled from the womb, cut off from our umbilical cord and breathing on our own, we have a separate identity such as we have never had before. We are not part of our mother. We aren't part of anyone else, either. Nor are we part of our environment — the air around us, other species, people of other times and places than our own. As we live on, we become more and more aware of this separate identity. When we pass from adolescence to adulthood we make a declaration of independence. We break many of the ties that we had with other people and places in order to take up a life of our own. We leave behind the portion of our life that we have already lived, never to get it back again. The title of Thomas Wolfe's great novel says it all: *You Can't Go Home Again*.

Other animals experience a similar separation from their parents and their world, a similar independence when they become adults. They don't seem to be aware of it as we are, or to feel it as deeply as we do. And they also don't have a very important remedy for their isolation that we have: intimacy, which allows us to live "in" each other, and thus be less lonely and isolated, even when we are physically apart. Intimacy comes about through love, and not in any other way. Let's take a look at exactly how this happens. It all begins in our mind, that wonderful power we have to stretch ourselves beyond ourselves, to be someone else psychologically while we still keep our original identity. Remember playing house, or playing school, when we were children? We'd say things like, "You be the Mom and I'll be the Dad," or "I want to be the teacher this time. You got to be the teacher last time." In our minds, we can be almost anything we want. We can travel to distant places —"Sorry, I was a thousand miles away. What did you say?" We can recapture our past, relive our memories, fantasize our future. Best of all, thanks to language, we can share each other's thought-worlds. I can let you in on my own private universe, and you can bring me into yours.

Our minds, then, are a wonderful way to overcome loneliness and isolation, to fill up, or fulfill, the emptiness we feel at being separate individuals. One of the ancient Greek philosophers even said that the perfection of a person lies in possessing the entire universe within himself, through knowing it.

Of course this is a somewhat figurative way of speaking. We cannot really hold the world inside our heads. We hold our ideas of it. That way of expanding ourselves is better than no way at all. But we have something else that is even better — love. When we love, we come into communion with our beloved in a real way, not just a figurative one. And loving communion with a spouse, in sexual passion, is a sacrament of communion with the rest of mankind as well as with the Three Divine Persons. What, exactly, is this love play which brings us into the love play of the Trinity? It won't happen unless we take care to make the symbol accurate. Our love must really represent divine love. Only then will it be able to cause it. What then, are the main features of love?

The first is union, the joining of two (or more) separate persons into one. But how can that be? When people love, they are still the people they were before, aren't they? They keep their individual identities, and even, if they wish, their original names, don't they? Well, yes and no. We have to clarify a few points before we can give a simple answer to that question. In fact, what is special about love is somewhat mysterious. Love is a way for two people to become one without ceasing to be two. A Persian mystic in the middle ages put it rather well: "A lover looks at his beloved and says, 'Myself!'" Married people will jokingly refer to a spouse as "My better half". And that little joke has a kernel of truth to it.

The key to understanding the union that comes about in love is this: to love someone is to wish what is good for him, to wish it to him for his sake, and then to look upon it as your own good. It sounds complicated, but it is something we do many times a day without even thinking about it. And the result of such love is that both persons, the lover and the beloved, both possess some good in common. They don't both possess it in the same way, but they do both possess it. And that common possession of a single good is what makes them one with each other. That is true whether they feel any special closeness or not. In fact, mundane jobs like directing traffic, selling groceries, or collecting garbage can be loving activities which bring about intimacy—if only people go about them in a loving way. On the other hand, what looks like close intimacy may not be so at all. People can live close to each other without love, and when they do, they have no intimacy, no communion at all. In the case of sacramental couples, their love has a special sexual quality which we will give a lot more attention to later. For now, let's just say that sexual intimacy is sacramental. It doesn't just bring the couple into union with each other; it also draws them into the love play of the Trinity.

Let's look at a few examples, to make the unifying power of love more evident. The first requirement of love is that the person who is doing the loving, the lover, must identify with the one loved, the beloved. For example, think of a loving wife washing her husband's shirts. There are several different attitudes she might have in mind while doing such a task. She could, of course, be full of resentment and a feeling of being used. Or she might do the laundry quite willingly, but out of some selfish motive, such as a desire to smugly display her housekeeping skills so as to make a neighbor jealous. In neither of these cases do we see any love, nor any intimacy or communion with her husband. She might just as well be a hired laundress. Her work is not nuptial and, if these attitudes are typical, neither is her life. Nothing sacramental there.

But let us suppose a wife who is madly, passionately in love. Without even thinking about it, she identifies with her husband. That is, she takes him as her other self. She cares about his welfare as her own — not *as if,* but *as* her own. She makes his good her good. And she wants him to have what is good for him — clean shirts, in this case — for his sake, not her own. The result is a new communion between her and her beloved husband. Both now possess a single good in common: the clean shirts. True, they don't both possess that good in the same way. The husband wears the shirts, and enjoys the physical and psychological benefits of wearing them. But — and here is the simple key to all human intimacies — those benefits belong to the wife, too. She can look at his health and welfare, at all the benefits he gains from his clean shirts, and say, "those goods are my goods, too". And they are hers, because she has chosen to make them so. This is the power of love, its unifying power.

Notice that we did not say that the wife gets certain benefits of her own from laundering those shirts. She does, of course, but those are beside the point. She gets a certain pride and satisfaction in work well done. She feels a certain pleasure and sense of accomplishment, and takes delight in looking at her beloved in his clean shirts. But these are not the goods we are talking about. What counts is that her husband's benefits from the clean shirts are also her good, so that she and he both possess the same good. That is what makes them one with each other, while they still remain two individual persons. They have assumed a new common identity. She is one with him because his good is her good, his self is her self. And these are hers because she has freely chosen to make them hers, to care about her husband's good as her own. So, the intimacy happens even if he doesn't return her love. Of course, in the best marriage, the love is mutual. In those cases, intimacy is doubled. For the husband takes his wife's good as his, and she takes his good as hers, and so the bond between them is doubled. Intimacy is made of a network of many such bonds, woven through repeated renewals of the love that originally drew the two together in the wish to live such a life together.

Some people might think — especially if they are taken in by some of the false ideas of the women's movement — that it is degrading for a woman to launder her husband's shirts. Housework is looked on as a kind of servitude or slavery. Women who care for men, and do so lovingly, are seen as putting themselves down, almost as masochists. Actually, the opposite is true. It is a distinctive belief of Christians, well-phrased in the Prayer for Peace of St. Francis: "It is in giving that we receive." We do not sacrifice ourselves when we love. We don't give ourselves up, or give ourselves away, making someone else more important. We find fulfillment for ourselves, expansion of our beings, a new fullness of life when we love. It is a paradox, to be sure, but it is true: the way to truly love myself, to make myself exist more fully, is by taking someone else as my other self, and loving that other person for his or her sake. Then I own two goods, my own and what I cherish in my beloved. If I don't care for any good except my own, then that is all I have. I remain isolated in my own private self when my love is centered there. And as Confucius said (on the comic pages, anyway), "A man all wrapped up in himself makes a mighty small package."

For example let's look at a passionate husband. Let's say that David finishes high school and is fortunate enough to find a job at the local bank. The job has a future, for he is told at the start that he will have the chance to work his way up to the top level. He works for several years, gradually learning new skills and being promoted to higher positions. And then one summer he announces that he is to be married during his vacation. When he returns, he goes to his desk to catch up on the work which had accumulated while he was gone. He continues to do the same things he was doing before his wedding. Or does he? He is still the same David that he was before he left. Or is he? It all depends on what is going on in David's mind. Maybe he thinks of his marriage as the ceremony in which he and his bride exchanged vows, then he comes back to work and picks up where he left off. Many men think this way. A wedding is the end of a process of wooing and winning a woman that has somewhat interrupted their life for a time. Such a husband is the same person, coming back to do the same work as he did before, picking up exactly where he left off. He is like the man that St. James describes, who takes a look at himself in the mirror and then goes on as if everything was still the same as before. He hasn't realized who he is.

But suppose David were passionate and tender, tender because he was passionate, passionate because he was tender. He would, without even trying, identify with his beloved wife. His wedding (actually, his falling in love, even before his wedding) would have moved the center of his whole life. He would no longer be wrapped up in himself. Instead, he would take his bride as his other self, her welfare as his. And in so identifying with her, he would want her to have what is good for her, for her sake. His work at the bank, then, would be utterly transformed. He would have Elaine constantly on his mind, as the be-all and end-all of everything he did. His work would be a way to support her and their life together. It would enable him to give her what she needed for her happiness — not just the things that money can buy. These are important, but more important is David's development as a person. His work would help him grow into a new self that he would share completely with Elaine. He would be a sacramental person to all he would meet. Does he have to interview a loan prospect? The fact that he is married, no longer his own person but Elaine's, would affect the way that he conducts such interviews. His motivation is different. His tenderness, his love for everyone, would be evident to all.

Do we mean to say, then, that passion changes the way people work, changes the occupation by which they earn their living? Yes, we do mean to say that. The sacrament of matrimony changes everything we do. That is because it changes our self-image, the way in which we think of ourselves. Our self-image goes with us wherever we go, and so it affects everything we do. The reason why matrimony changes our way of thinking about ourselves is that it changes our very selves. It gives us new, coupled identities. In fact, it would be very appropriate for people to change their names when they get married. The old custom of women taking their husbands' names has been criticized, and many women now choose not to do so. If they have a professional reputation before they marry, they may keep their maiden names in order to continue that reputation. But when a woman chooses to be called Mrs. _____, taking on her husband's family name, she is making a very profound statement about her new identity. She is no longer the detached, self-possessed individual that she once was. She is now somebody's, someone's beloved, belonging to him. Her use of his name is a way of recognizing that new identity, and of asking others to recognize it, too. Wouldn't it be better, though, if husbands also took on new names to signify their new belonging? Not their wife's family name, perhaps, for that would create a lot of confusion. Perhaps a new name for both would signal their new shared identities. We do take on names at baptism and confirmation, and titles such as *Doctor* and *Esquire* when we enter certain professions. The taking on of new marital names by both spouses would signal a change in identities that is deeper than any of these others.

When David returns to his desk, then, he has a new identity, even though our society does not have a title for him which would make that identity clear. His new identity is an intimate coupled one, which leaves him no longer the isolated, self-possessed individual that he was before he fell in love. Does his work at the bank allow him to buy Elaine a new stereo? If so, the pleasure that she finds in it is his pleasure, too. And in that joint possession of a single good—Elaine's pleasure as she feels it, David's identification with it as his own—they are united in a loving intimacy. That intimacy is true whether David takes any pleasure of his own in the stereo or not. And it is true even if, in a sad case, Elaine does not return his love. But in a sacramental marriage she will, of course, love him as much as he loves her, thus forging bonds of intimacy to match his so that they gradually build the web of a shared identity.

The paradox stated by Jesus is perfectly true, then: he that loses his life shall find it, while he who seeks to keep his life will lose it indeed. Selfishness blocks our fulfillment because it keeps us wrapped up in ourselves. "Where your heart is, there also is your treasure." But we find fulfillment when we step out of ourselves by loving someone else, by looking at another person and saying, "Hello, self!" We are not just saying that if you love people, they will love you back. In the first place, this is often untrue. But even when it is, such an exchange of love is not always intimate, and not always sacramental. We are talking about something much deeper than the fulfillment which psychologists and psychiatrists recommend. People do feel better, and seem to be healthier and more mature, when they enjoy intimacy with other people. To say the very least, life is much more interesting that way. Certainly selfish and withdrawn people have few friends, and seem to be unhappy.

But the stakes are much higher than that. When we speak of sex as sacramental, as love, that most masterful passion, making people believe in immortality, we are speaking of people being saved from sin and death. We are speaking of building up the Body of Christ, the Church. Our search for intimacy is, quite literally, a matter of life and death. Does it seem unimportant whether a wife does the laundry with the fire of sexual passion burning in her heart? Does it really matter whether a banker fills out his forms with his urgency for his wife glowing in the back of his mind? It does, indeed. It makes the difference between sex, which is a sacrament, and marriage which is a contract and which can so easily be a dead issue. When our lives become accurate symbols of the love play of the Trinity, they cause what they symbolize. We do not, then, just contemplate the life of God as outside observers. We do not imitate it, or seek it as an ideal. We take part in it.

Have you ever known a homeowner who had foundation problems? Of all the things that can go wrong with a house, cracks, bulges, cave-ins and other defects in the foundation cause the greatest dismay. The reason is the foundation is just that, a foundation to the rest of the house. If someone has plumbing, roofing, or electrical problems, he still has a house. Those other problems can be solved. But if his foundation collapses, then he also has plumbing, roofing and electrical problems as well. And these cannot be solved, because his house is no more. He needs to start over with another house on another foundation.

Intimacy is the foundation of our life in the Church. We may have many faults and weaknesses, but as long as we sincerely try to love, our other problems can be solved, our weaknesses can be healed. For in seeking intimacy, we have our intimacy with God. But let that intimacy collapse, let us stop loving and trying to love, and everything else collapses, too. There is no healing of other faults until our basic love is restored. And for couples, that love is sex—tender passion, passionate tenderness. The sacrament of sex is quite literally a matter of life and death:

> I call heaven and earth to witness against you today. I set before you life or death, blessing or curse. Choose life, then, so that you and your descendants may live, in the love of Yahweh your God, obeying his voice, clinging to him; for in this your life consists. . . (Dt 30, 19-20)

CHAPTER TWO

Sex Is Passion

You made me love you, I didn't want to do it, I didn't want to do it. You made me want you, and all the time you knew it. I guess you always knew it.
You made me happy, you made me sad.
And there were times, dear you made me feel so bad.

The words of this song refer to a sacramental symbol: sex. While they don't tell the whole story, one very important part is there. Sex is a grace, the grace of a vocation. It is a divine gift — unearned, perhaps unasked for. It is given freely by the Spirit, Who "breathes where he will". St. Augustine described it in a classic phrase: grace, he said, is "done in us, without us." I often see grace at work in my life — those times when, after a long struggle to love, I finally have some success. And the success is always a surprise. The loving I do is not the loving I was trying to do. My struggle seems necessary, as some sort of prelude to the success. But the power to really love someone comes as a gift. It is always a surprise. It often makes me feel like the character in a play who suddenly discovered he had been speaking prose all his life, and didn't even know it.

Sex is a most obvious grace, though, a startlingly clear and dramatic gift from God. For when people love in the way that we have been speaking of (remember Webster's definition? "A tender, passionate affection for one of the opposite sex"), they know it at once. And so does everyone who has any dealings with them. We want to look now, at two particularly luminous moments of that grace which we are calling *sex*. These two moments are highly sacramental, because they are so clear and dramatic. They shout out loud and clear to anyone who is in shouting distance: "Love is here. And since God is Love, God is here, too."

These two moments are falling (and then being) in love, and sexual intercourse. Is it unusual to think of sexual intercourse as a sacrament?

The Church has always made it a necessary condition for a fully valid, sacramental marriage. Impotent people cannot be married. They may live together, or be close friends. They may develop a very wonderful friendship, a Christian intimacy. But they are not married and, if the impotence is permanent, never can be. In fact, when fully functioning couples marry, until their wedding ceremony is ratified in sexual intercourse, their marriage can be legally dissolved. So may a celibate marriage be dissolved. Such a marriage was that of Jacques and Raissa Maritain, in which both parties were capable of sexual activity, but refrained from it by mutual agreement.

One of my students was very surprised by this requirement. She said, "I never thought the Church would put so much emphasis on sex." But the Church does put that emphasis on sex and, if we think about it a bit, we can see why. But let's look first at where it all begins — the experience of falling in love.

> Some enchanted evening
> You will see a stranger
> You will see a stranger
> Across a crowded room
> And somehow you know,
> You know even then,
> That somehow you'll see him,
> Again and again.

It does often happen through a meeting of the eyes. But even when it comes in some other way — through the mail, perhaps, or over the telephone — there comes that moment when something is "done in us without us." The common expression we use, *falling* in love, indicates that it is something we do not initiate and cannot control. We can arrange for people to meet each other. But we cannot make anyone fall in love. We cannot, ourselves, fall in love when and with whom we choose. And we cannot make any other person fall in love with us or with someone else either.

This quality of being in love is essential for a marriage that is fully sacramental, one that is a clear revelation of the love play of the Trinity. We mentioned earlier how sacraments cause what they symbolize, precisely by symbolizing it. The symbol, then, must be accurate. We cannot baptize with soup or muddy water, for example. The cleansing symbol would not be clear. People would not read the symbol correctly, and its causal power would be weakened, too. Someone asked a theologian friend of mine one day whether we might use, for the Eucharist, food and drink which are more typical of our culture. Specifically, could we have a Eucharist with, say, Coke and pizza? His answer was negative: "No. I think that the symbolism of intoxication is very central to the Eucharist. We are to be in love with Christ, His Father, and His Spirit the way the apostles were on the first Pentecost. People who saw them thought they were drunk." Even so, a married couple have to be sexual all the time. Once they fall in love they have to stay there, and even fall farther; otherwise their symbol will be obscured.

But what, exactly, is so special about being in love? What is the reality, the interpersonal reality, that this little three-letter word, S*E*X, refers to? We certainly know it when we see it. In fact, we could say about sex what St. Augustine once said about time: "I know perfectly well what it is—until someone asks me to put it into words." But let's try our best. What is it that we notice when we see a sexy, passionate, loving couple? They have a special aura about their whole way of acting with and speaking to each other. When they meet, they don't say a casual, distracted "hello." When they part, their farewells are not routine and mechanical. Their mannerisms, their speech, their tone of voice all make it clear that they see each other as very special persons indeed. Their being together is exciting. Their being apart is painful. They can spend hours in conversation, go to their separate homes, and immediately spend more hours together over the telephone. And even when they are talking about mundane things, such as paying bills, making appointments, the weather forecast, their talk has sexual overtones to it that are obvious to anyone who happens to overhear them. Everything they say and do bespeaks passion, affection, excitement.

Couples who are in love exude an aura. They attract attention by the intensity of their feeling for each other. Their life is continuous love play. Take an average day sometime and spend an hour or so in people-watching. Sit on a park bench, or stroll on a campus or shopping mall and watch for male-female pairs. It won't be hard to tell which ones are just friends and which have just met casually. We can recognize staid long-married couples, those who are kind and pleasant to each other, but basically unexcited about each other and about life in general. And then let a pair of lovers come on the scene. We can spot them at once. The way they look at each other, the way they walk together—their body language reveals who they are. If we could listen to their conversation, we would hear them speak to each other differently than they do to others. When apart, they would speak about each other differently, too. When I was in college, rooming with several other girls, we always did a "post mortem" when someone came in from a date. But when a girl came in all aglow, and didn't want to take part in that kind of conversation, we knew things were getting serious. Lovers respect each other's privacy and do not talk critically behind each other's backs.

When lovers do speak to others, they habitually, and easily, use the word "we" instead of "I." They don't talk about their rights, about what their beloveds owe them. They're not constantly on the alert to see whether they are being treated fairly or not. And their body language speaks volumes when they are together. They seek eye contact, rather than avoiding it. (One of the stories told about the Maritains is that whenever they were in a philosophical conversation with a group, and someone would ask Jacques for his opinion, he always looked at Raissa before he answered.) Lovers exchange glances that are knowing rather than questioning. They tease and flirt, with eyes and lips, even at a distance. They are constantly alert to each other's thoughts and feelings, instantly responsive to each other's slightest touch. They lean toward each other, and face each other, instead of turning away. Their speech is not hurried and anxious, but relaxed and slow and gentle. They might hold hands, and when they do, it is not in a mechanical, forced, or distracted fashion, but warm and eager. Even though we never see them make love, or don't even know whether they have, we would know, by these many signs, that they are in love.

The point is that they have a special awareness of themselves and of each other because they have a special relationship that truly constitutes a new identity for them. They think of themselves differently because they *are* different, and that new thinking comes out even in their smallest, unconscious gestures. What is the difference? It is unity. Something has tied these previously separate individuals together so that they are now, in some sense, one. They are no longer the persons they once were. They belong to each other. And their top priority, because of this new belonging, is to be together as constantly and as closely as they can. They want to be in each other's company as much as possible, and when they must be apart, they want to be in each other's minds and hearts.

Their sexual desire is the spark that sets off their relationship from all others. Mary knows, likes, and admires many other men, and Joe many other women. Both know other good people whom they enjoy as friends, whom they could be reasonably happy with as spouses, even. But there is a special urgency about their feeling for each other, a sexual spark, which they don't feel with their other friends. That spark of sex is what changes their identities, binds them together, makes them belong to each other as they belong to no one else in the world.

Once that spark is struck between them, they simply are not the people they once were. No one can identify them independently of each other. Who is Mary? She is no longer the attorney in Children's Court. She is Joe's woman. She has many character traits that we could describe her by. But the most important fact about her is her tie to Joe, and the passion that gives that tie its roots. And who is Joe? Friends no longer identify him as they once did—that university student down the block, or the worker on the third machine. He is Mary's man, her beloved, her lover. That fact is what defines his life, in his eyes, in her eyes, and in everyone else's eyes. He is unique in all the world, unlike any other man, because he belongs, in his passion, to her. This new belonging even takes precedence over their family relationships. Mary is still John and Martha's daughter, of course, and Judy's sister, and Helen's niece, and Gerald's cousin. But these belongings are not the primary ones for her—not anymore. She is Joe's beloved and, oh yes, also the daughter of John and Martha, and so on. And we can say the same for Joe. Falling in love is the first step toward the creation of a new family, and the lovers belong to that new family, even more deeply than they belong to their original families, from the first moment of their acknowledging and accepting their passion for each other.

What we are referring to, then, is the sacramental symbol of matrimony, the passionate devotion, devoted passion, passion, desire, love, urgency, intimacy, personal presence—in short, sex—that makes marriage a luminous revelation and cause of the presence of God. The symbol is that reality which we recognize at once when we fall in love or know someone else who does. It seems artificial, even silly, to describe love in words. In fact, young people often ask (and older ones, too) in their letters to advice columns, "How do I know if I am in love?" The only honest answer to that question is, "If you're wondering, you're not." The experience is so intense and dramatic that there is no doubt when it happens. But it is worth a bit of analysis, for if we believe it to be a sacrament and instrument of salvation, then we want to cultivate and nurture it, to make the most of it. We want to be of it (a little) more careful than of everything. And that means some measure of conscious effort, in which we know what we are doing. The grace comes as a gift, of course. It is not at our command. But like any other grace, any success in loving, it calls for our best effort. We have to accept it by a conscious choice.

Sex, then, as the mark of lovers, is a newly heightened awareness and newly intense feelings. But these feelings, and this awareness, are rooted in a new reality, the unity between two persons who were formerly quite separate from each other. Now they belong to each other. That unity is the grace of vocation. A couple who are drawn together in this way experience a force beyond their own control. It is something which happens to them, rather than something that they do — although once it does happen to them, they decide whether or not to accept it. But once they accept that force of attraction, their whole perspective of life is changed. They now see everything — each other and all the rest of life — through a sexual prism. People often wonder what lovers see in each other. But the lovers wonder why everyone else doesn't see what they see. What happens is that passion focuses their attention on each other's goodness. They don't deny each other's faults, or create illusions. But they put the faults into perspective, as a distant background to the goodness that draws their love.

In ancient Greek and Roman art, Cupid was pictured blindfolded. And we have the proverb, "Love is blind." Such proverbs do not come out of nowhere. They have a basis in human experience. But the blindness of love is not so much a blindness as a selective vision. The good that lovers see in each other is really there — it is not an illusion. But others do not see it because they do not have the advantage of the sexual prism, the passion and desire, which draws lovers to each other. Thanks to the perspective of sexual desire, lovers find their attention riveted on what is good and attractive in each other. Faults and weaknesses, even some very serious ones, may be seen, too. But in the context of such goodness they lose their power to discourage and repel.

Of course there are tragic cases of infatuation. Sometimes an immature, sentimental feeling does create illusions, does deny faults, and draws people together who ought not to be so drawn. Infatuated people have no capacity for intimacy and devotion. Such adolescent pairings (and they are adolescent, even when the people involved are older) are not what we have in mind. We are speaking of a certain chemistry which draws two clear-eyed adults together in mutual devotion and ecstasy. The difference here is evident: in sentimental, immature infatuations, each person seeks his own benefit. He is drawn to her because she makes him happy, makes him feel good. Or she is drawn to him for the same reasons. But sacramental sex urges people to a totally generous self-abandoning devotion to each other's welfare. Thus an infatuated girl will be drawn to a boy because he takes her to her favorite restaurant, buys her expensive presents, gives her something to brag about to her friends. With the loving couples we are describing, their passion is a grace that lures them out of such selfishness into an almost ridiculous generosity. We can see such lovers quarrelling over where to go on a date, what kind of pizza to order, which music to listen to — not because each is trying to have his or her own way, but because each truly prefers the preferences of the other.

> I should stay away,
> But what can I do?
> I hear your name,
> And I'm aflame . . .
> For you're the lover
> I have waited for
> The mate that Fate
> Had me created for . . .

When couples trace the events which led up to their falling in love, they usually find a whole series of coincidences, of chance meetings here and there, of people taking one path rather than another—a whole chain of events which might not have happened at all. The meeting at which my husband and I fell in love would not have happened if the Andrea Doria hadn't sunk, even though neither of us was on that ship. It led to a series of coincidences which brought us together in an experience of "that Old Black Magic". When lovers do meet, however, their coming together seems so right that it is almost inevitable. It is as if something—or Someone— who knows better than we do what is good for us is running the world. The Old Black Magic is, of course, not Fate, but the Providence of God. All human relationships, not just marriages, are made in heaven.

It is a paradox that two people can become one with each other. It sounds like a contradiction. One of the Greek poets once said that lovers would like to merge with each other physically, but they realize that such a merger would destroy one (or both!) and so they seek the next best thing: they live together, sharing thoughts and feelings, doing things together. Some of the common expressions we hear show how intense that desire for unity is. Think how often, in speaking our love, we use words connected with eating: "I love you so much I could eat you up!" We use terms of endearment that refer to our sense of taste: "Honey," "Sweetheart." We hug as tightly as we can, almost as if we wanted to "melt" into each other. And the act of kissing has deep significance. It is really an exchange of breath, the breath of life—symbolizing the exchange of lives, of our very selves, that we would like to make. Some primitive people seem to have practiced cannibalism with such symbolism in mind. They were not fierce warriors devouring the flesh of their enemies in an act of supreme hostility. Rather, in a very careful and delicate ritual, they ate the bodies of their dead parents and relatives as a sign of their desire that those loved ones would continue to be present to them.

Thomas Aquinas—that medieval monk who never had a lover— has a beautiful description of the kind of unity that lovers experience.

He calls it "mutual indwelling". And the bonds created by love are four in number. First, the beloved lives in the lover's mind, as a constant preoccupation. Isn't that true? When someone has fallen in love, it is sometimes hard to get his attention. He has something else — someone else — on his mind. His life has a new center. The second bond is the lover's effort to enter the mind of his beloved, to find out all his beloved's deepest thoughts and feelings, memories and hopes. To love someone is to be totally fascinated by him or her. Everything about the beloved is interesting, everything he or she thinks is an infallible opinion. Suddenly the world has a new authority on everything!

The next two bonds are in the lover's feelings, too — they tie him to his beloved. Third, there is the matter of his own feelings. One who is in love has a whole new set of feelings that he has never had before. He feels new joys and sorrows, new fears and hopes, sometimes new anger or despair. And all of these feelings are due to one single fact: his or her love for another person. When we fall in love, our feelings are caused by our beloved. We would not have them otherwise. And those feelings are our beloved's presence in us, his or her power operating in us, to make us different from what we would be otherwise.

Feelings create the fourth bond, too. One who is in love identifies with the feelings of his beloved. When my husband is upset, elated, angry, hopeful, I don't want to know merely that he has those feelings. My curiosity is not that of an outside observer. No, anyone who is in love feels his beloved's feelings as his own. If Ed is angry or joyous, I feel angry or joyous, too, and for the same reasons. Lovers don't just observe each other's reactions, values and decisions: they make them their own.

Thomas Aquinas described these four psychological bonds that tie lovers together. But this is only half the story, for these bonds come about when only one person loves and the other doesn't reciprocate. When the other *does* reciprocate — when the love is mutual — then these bonds are doubled. Each person is the other's lover, each is the other's beloved, and each dwells in the other's mind and affections in these four ways. Then their unity, their belonging to each other, is doubly tight, doubly strong. Thomas Aquinas has done nothing more than describe what we all instantly recognize when we see a couple who are in love, or when we have fallen in love ourselves. It is not infatuation, but fascination. In fact, a graduate student in philosophy put it rather well to one of my friends. This sad young man — not yet thirty, and already divorced twice — said, "I think what it takes to make a marriage work is fascination. You have to be so utterly fascinated with the other person that you want to know everything there is to know about him or her."

Fascination — not with self, but with another. That one word sums up what makes sex sacramental. Sex is a God-given power which draws our minds and hearts away from ourselves. Is anything more central to loving as Jesus loved? Isn't the fascination that lovers experience just one form of loving our neighbor as ourself? Surely, as long as we remain fascinated with ourselves, we will not love anyone. We won't even notice that other people exist. We'll just take them for granted, in an absent-minded sort of way, except when we want to get something out of them. I mentioned to one of my confessors one day that I often had the experience of hurting someone, without really meaning to, by some thoughtless remark or action. And then when I see the hurt I suddenly realize, to my dismay, that this is a *person* — someone with feelings, someone precious and mysterious. And this realization makes me regret my thoughtlessness immediately. "Yes," said the priest, "I've experienced that myself." "But why?" I asked, "Why can't we have more of that realization ahead of time, so that we won't do thoughtless, hurtful things?" "I don't know," he replied. "I guess we just don't have it all together yet." For many years, I have felt anguished by my not "getting it all together" any better than I have. But recently I've seen a more positive side to this phenomenon: at least my unintentional hurts to other people do sometimes bring me to a realization of their goodness. Then I see them as persons and I am making a step forward in loving my neighbor as myself. Realization after a hurt is better than no realization at all.

This need to realize that people are people, not just shapes in the background of our own fascinating selves, is something that all of us have. Our fascination with ourselves has to be broken somehow and turned into a fascination with other people (who really are, by the way, fascinating). Therefore we should be thankful for it whenever and however it happens. Sexual desire is one of the world's most powerful energies for bringing about this conversion. I am sure that without my passion for my husband (and his for me), my fascination with myself would be even more intense than it is. For falling in love is a first giant step outward toward another person. I have passionate days, and less passionate ones. On those days when my passion is strong, my sexual desire intense — those blessed days when I seem to have fallen in love all over again — I find all other people fascinating. I notice them, enjoy them, easily wish them well. Those are the days when I am sure the grace of the sacrament of matrimony is at work in me.

The sexual aura of couples who are in love is one especially bright and clear moment of God's revelation. Another, even more bright and clear, even explosive moment, is the ecstasy of sexual intercourse. How, you might be wondering, can intercourse be sacramental? How can it be a symbol or revelation when it is such a private act? The wedding ceremony, yes — that's a public ritual, and everyone can see and hear the couple's expression of their love. But what they do in the bedroom, we don't think or fantasize about. That's too private. The Church does, though, make intercourse necessary for the wedding ceremony to be complete. So, there is something very important about that action, something which speaks of the inner life of God. Sexual intercourse says something, and what it says is the same as what the moment of falling in love says. It says unity, passion, fascination, intimacy. It says love, tenderness, devotion. It says personal presence and mutual indwelling. It says sex. But intercourse says all of these in a uniquely dramatic way. There is, quite simply, no other human activity that has such power and drama. Sexual ecstasy is the high point, the peak experience, of being in love.

Why is that? In the Middle Ages, the Church began to emphasize a view of marriage that was quite different from what the society around her had practiced. The new emphasis was on love and romance. Previously, marriage was seen as a contract in which the spouses often had little to say. Marriages were arranged by parents, and men and women were often joined together for political or economic reasons that had little to do with love and romance. It was hoped that a couple might fall in love after they were married, and often enough they did. But it was not common, until the Church began to make it so, for people to choose their own partners because they were already in love. Romantic attraction — the fascination we have spoken of — was not a widely accepted reason for two people to marry, until the Church made it so. Love was then made a part of the sacramental symbol. In fact, the Church put a special emphasis on love: couples who had a tender and passionate devotion to and affection for each other, but chose to abstain from sexual intercourse, were considered to have exemplary marriages. A legal contract, along with physically complete but unloving sexual activity, was not her ideal.

Celibate marriage was not her ideal, either. Love without intercourse was better than intercourse without love, but a marriage in the fullest sense of the term — fully sacramental, one that could not be dissolved — brought spouses together in loving intercourse. And if we look at such loving intercourse for a moment, we can see why it is such an appropriate sacramental symbol. It draws attention, of course, as any sacrament must do. Whether or not people have ever had sexual intercourse is one of the most important facts we want to know about them. That fact tells us how to relate to them, what we can and cannot say to them, what they know and do not know, realize and do not realize. The first experience of intercourse changes a person permanently, because it is so powerful. What is so special about this action? Why does it have such power? Why is it uniquely suited to be a revelation and cause of love, a sacrament? To put it as concretely as we can, how does sexual intercourse, the culmination of love play, bespeak the presence of God?

The reason is ecstasy. Ecstasy means, literally, "stepping outside of oneself." That sounds odd, doesn't it? How can someone step outside of himself? Yet, we do. We speak of people being "beside themselves" with grief, or joy. We speak of them "not being themselves" because of a grouchy mood. All of these expressions try to say something about us that is strange but true: our minds can, in some mysterious way, step out of our bodies. For example, when we are dreaming of far away places we say, "I'm sorry—I didn't hear you. I was 1000 miles away." Ecstasy, then, is a psychological stepping outside of our own skins, a decentering of our minds and wills from ourselves toward someone else. It is a kind of self-forgetting. Now, any kind of love requires us to do that to some extent. We wouldn't ordinarily think of doing the laundry as an ecstatic action (except when paid models do it in the TV commercials). But it is, in a way. A woman who washes her husband's shirts, for example, cannot have her mind totally on herself and her own needs. She has to move her attention, her consciousness, away from herself at least enough to realize that her husband needs some clean shirts. Her affection shifts, too. Instead of being totally concerned for herself, and putting her effort and energy toward some need of her own, she displaces these toward another person—her husband.

All of this is true even if the wife is not especially passionate. Even when we do loving things for someone out of a dry, mechanical sense of duty, our minds and hearts are taken out of us, to some extent, and centered on the person whose needs we are serving. Now, if the wife we are speaking of is still in love, still has that fascination with her spouse that we spoke of earlier, then her ecstasy is more intense. She will "step out of herself" with more feeling and energy, more enthusiasm and joy, perhaps even awe—depending on how intense her realization is at that moment.

But even the ecstasy we feel at the height of passion in our daily household tasks is pale and feeble in comparison to the ecstasy of sexual intercourse. And, just to balance our examples, the ecstasy of a loving husband at the moment of his sexual release is worlds beyond what he feels in any of his other moments of excited romance. His heart may sing while he works at his desk, as he thinks of the beloved for whom he does his work, the one to whom he belongs in the passion that first drew them together. But that song in his heart is as nothing compared to the ecstasy of their making love. What is so special about orgasm?

What is special about orgasm is the intensity, the totality, of the ecstasy. In every other loving action, no matter how absorbed we are in the person that we're doing it for, we still keep some of our attention and awareness to ourselves. The wife who fairly floats to the basement to wash her husband's shirts, for example, knows in some fringe of her consciousness who she is, where she is, what she is doing. The husband who goes about his job in a passionate preoccupation with his beloved also keeps his control. He is well aware of who and where he is, perfectly able to give his attention to the details of his work. But when the two explode into orgasm for a few moments, at least, their minds are totally decentered from themselves. They lose all awareness of who they are, and where they are, what they are doing. They "step out of themselves" in a uniquely total way.

Orgasm also decenters people's hearts, wills, and feelings. Again, in any lesser ecstasy—as that of the passionate laundress, or of the sexually urgent accountant—people keep their control. They are in command of their bodies, of their voluntary muscles. They act and speak as they choose, even though the center of their speaking and action is not themselves but their beloveds. But in orgasm, every last shred of control is lost. At that moment, lovers no longer control, no longer even wish to control, their words and actions. They babble and scream, thrash about, in total abandon, doing and saying things they would never dream of doing and saying when they are calm. In fact, isn't such abandon the whole point of intercourse? Intercourse is the body language *par excellence* of ecstasy, of self-abandon, of unity and mutual indwelling, of intimacy. Nothing else in the whole world says, in such a dramatically clear and vivid fashion, "I can't resist you, I can't hold back. I am eager to give you my entire self, and to take your gift of yourself to me." As Eric Berne said, in his *Sex and Human Loving*, we don't need a lot of words when we make love—four will do. These words are "Please," "Thank You," "Ugh!" and "Wow!" The "Wow! is the one that counts, the one that all the others lead up to.

The ecstasy of orgasm, brief as it is, is the symbol and culmination of many other realities. It shows better than anything else imaginable that two people are in love. In it, the passionate devotion that they live in so many other ways reaches a certain high point. No other gesture we can think of says more clearly that two people are joined together as one, that they long for a belonging and unity that is as total as anything human can be. But as Catholics, we can see a special value, a special reason for the Church to "put so much emphasis on sex". For the "Wow!" of orgasm is a "Wow!" to divine life. Sex is a sacramental power, not just a human action. It is the power to cause God's own life in us, to draw us into the love play of the Trinity. And orgasm, as the high point of sexual love, is also one of love's most powerful divine moments. Primitive religions often include phallic worship as one of their important rituals. Such worship is not always coarse and degrading. It can be an affirmation of the power of human sexuality to give life to human beings. In fact, it was common among Renaissance painters to emphasize the genitals of the Infant Jesus, and of the Risen Christ as well. It was their way of saying, "Yes, look! He really did have what it takes to give life to human beings. Let's celebrate that fact."

When we see life, though, in a deeper sense than the biological, our form of "phallic worship" has a deeper meaning, too. For human beings as for no other animals, life is intimacy, love, communion, belonging to each other. Life is not physical existence. But it also is not just human intimacy, wondrous though that is. Our intimacy brings us close to God, to life in Him, to His life in us. And so, sex is indeed cause for celebration. Sex *is* celebration. "Greater love than this, no man has: that he lay down his life for his friend." When spouses, in orgasm and then in the rest of their life together, let themselves be totally overcome by each other's goodness, they are laying down their lives for each other, just as surely as if they stepped in front of an oncoming train.

In making sexual intercourse — or at least, the ability for it — a requirement for marriage, the Church tells us something about Jesus' command to all of us to love each other as He did. He loved, and loves, us with the same ecstatic abandon with which He loves His Father and Spirit, with which they love Him and each other. In the Trinity no one holds anything back. The Three Persons keep for themselves no shred of awareness, no iota of the energy of their divine being. They abandon everything to each other. Jesus abandons Himself to us in exactly the same way, and commands us to do the same for each other.

Love play, then, ought to be every Christian's constant state of being. But what can that mean? Only that the ecstasy, the self-abandon that reaches a peak in orgasm is to be acted out in all the circumstances of all our lives — not just in the private moments of making love. Those private moments are a model of how all of us should love all of us, all of the time. Of course, we're not recommending promiscuous intercourse. But we are recommending "promiscuous" love. We are called to abandon ourselves in some sort of total devotion to everyone we meet. Take a simple, almost embarrassing example: suppose we meet a casual acquaintance while we are out for a walk, and that person says, "Good morning.

Beautiful day, isn't it?" The response anyone would expect is "Yes, isn't it?" or some such words. And then we go our separate ways. But if we speak even those brief words to each other out of love, out of the love which Jesus has for us, the love play that circulates within the Trinity, there is ecstasy in that simple "Yes, isn't it?"

Any word of greeting to anyone, even a stranger, implies that we would lay down our life for that person. Everyone we meet is the neighbor whom we are to love as ourselves. All of life is different when we once begin to love as Jesus did, even our comments about the weather. For He loves with constant ecstatic desire to belong completely to those whom He loves. And so, spouses, in their sexual abandon, show the rest of us the way. There is only one way that is appropriate, for Christians to ex-change comments about the weather, or to have any other contact with each other. And that way is mirrored in sex. It is a passionate desire to belong to each other totally, to love each other with nothing held back. It is mutual self-abandon.

The great saints understood these matters. They did not, any of them, consider themselves saints. They considered themselves sinners. Great lovers that they were, they did not take pride in that fact. They thought they were failures in loving. Now, they were not putting them-selves down in some sort of false humility or masochism. They just realized more clearly than the rest of us the truly awesome life of intimacy that we are all called to. They realized, for example, that a moment's indifference, even to a stranger, is a failure in loving. Can a wife be in-different to her husband when in the throes of sexual ecstasy? Hardly. Can a husband remain preoccupied with himself in that moment of abandon? Of course not. Their utterly ecstatic, urgent, total gift of them-selves to each other is a sign, and model, of how they, and all the rest of us, are to love each other all the time. The saints knew that. They had some insight into what it means to give up our lives for our friends. They had some glimmer of realization of what it is like to love our neigh-bor as ourselves, to love our enemies, to do good to those who hate us. And where did they get that insight into love, that realization? From sex. Not from their own intercourse, in most cases, for most of them were not married. But from their parents, and whoever taught them how to love in their early lives. Later on, we will look at the causal power of sex, how it operates as an energy as well as a model. But for now, just seeing how sex, with intercourse as its high point, is a model of all of Christian life, we are looking at something awesome indeed. We have to wonder if the saints would have come to their insights into love, without the model, over the centuries, of spouses living in daily self-abandon.

Love-making and falling in love — these are two especially clear moments of sacramental sex. In both we find two people with heightened awareness of each other, and intense passion for each other. The energy of sexual desire is the source of self-abandon, a self-abandon which ought to be a constant state of being for spouses as for all Christians. Couples themselves thus make up the sacrament of matrimony. Their sacrament is not their wedding. The wedding is a public ritualizing of their sexual desire, of the oneness and belonging that flow from that desire as a river flows from melting snow in the mountains. The couples themselves are the sacrament. Their sexual way of life is an instrument by which Christ the Bridegroom prepares for Himself a bride without blemish, the Church.

Once we begin to see sacramental sex as a revelation of the life of the Trinity, a wonderful circle begins. The Trinity then begins to be a model for sacramental sex. This circle can happen in every part of human life. Human life is an image of the divine, and divine life is a model of the human. The two mirror each other. Anything we can learn about God, then, casts some light on human life as it ought to be. And *vice versa* — anything we learn about human life as it ought to be gives us some clues to the inner, hidden life of God. How can we see the life of Father, Son and Spirit mirrored in the sexual ecstasy of spouses? The most important insight is one that we have already mentioned briefly, that love is primarily intimate play, not ministry. Many people are mistaken on this point, probably because ministry is so essential to love that it is hard to look beyond it.

Ministry means attending to someone's needs. Certainly that is part of love. For, as Webster says so well, affection is part of love, and affection certainly means being stirred by the the wants and desires of those we love. It is only natural that we look to our beloved, see that he or she needs, wants, desires something, and then do our best to supply it. A great deal of human love consists in service to needs: providing food, clothing, shelter, education, entertainment to those we love. Indeed, it would be a poor lover — no lover at all, really — who would constantly gaze at his beloved in awe, and never do any of the work. But it would be an equally poor lover who never did anything except the work. My husband and I used to visit a relative who was constantly busy, anxiously doing things for us. We could appreciate that service, of course. But people can go too far in their busyness and miss the point of a visit. This person, a maiden aunt, would get up at 4 a.m. on Christmas to cook a dinner for us that even included plum pudding made from scratch. We went to Church without her, and she was too busy to talk to us during the day. In fact, during dinner, she was too busy serving to sit down and eat with us. She was giving us her ministry to the *nth* degree.

But there is more to love than service. In fact, service is only a means to an end. An anxious busyness really defeats the purpose of life. That purpose is intimacy, play—our simple enjoyment of each other in conversation and games. That is true in married life, and in all the rest of life as well. People who seek to serve others without having any personal intimacy with them are acting in a patronizing way, not a loving way. When I take no stance toward another person except that of seeing that he needs something, and then trying to provide it, I am not loving that person as Jesus did. The one I serve is not the neighbor whom I love as myself, but an inferior whom I lord it over. Couples can easily make that mistake. Their life is, in a way, a constant ministry to each other. Even conversation can be that—the communication of information which someone needs. But sometimes it is no more than that. Some couples go for days, even longer without talking about anything except the practical details of who is going to do what, when, and where. Even sexual intercourse can turn into a ministry, a favor that one does for the other. That favor is no small thing. We can make love in order to give each other some very important psychological benefits: release of tension, assurance of self-worth, pleasure. But a constant ministry is deadly to sex. Sex is intimacy, and intimacy is play.

Here's where our beliefs about the Trinity can help us. Can we picture three divine, utterly perfect persons living together in love? What would their love be like? It would not be, could not be, any kind of ministry. Being divine, they have no needs to be met. All the work, we might say, is done. They are together with nothing to do. But do they then do nothing? Well, in a way, yes. Their activity is something higher and better than mere doing. They contemplate each other. And, as one of my professors used to put it, the motto of contemplation is, "Don't just do something. Stand there." When we contemplate a sunset, or a perfect moment between two people who love each other, we don't want to do anything. Doing anything would spoil the moment, would be a distraction. We just want to enjoy what is there, to let it be in all its beauty. The life of the three divine persons is like that all the time—one long, eternal moment of contemplation. They see each other and exult in the good that they see, letting it be in all its beauty.

It may seem that such contemplation is less than a busy ministry to needs, but it is not. It is really more. Which is the greater love—what a mother has in her heart as she stays up all night laboring to care for a sick child? Or what she has in her heart when, years later, she and that child, now grown, spend an afternoon reminiscing over family snapshots, in simple enjoyment of their belonging to each other? Even so, the inner life of God is one of simple enjoyment, in which three persons see how they belong to each other and exult in that enjoyment. Their joy is ecstatic. As Father, Son and Spirit see each other's goodness, they are taken out of themselves in ecstatic enjoyment of what they see.

Their complete ecstasy shows us what our lives should be. It shows couples what their sexual intimacy ought to be, in bed and out. There is not the tiniest shred of the Father's identity that He holds back from His Son, nothing in Him that is not Father to that Son. His Fatherhood is not a role that He plays, now taking it up and now laying it down. His Fatherhood is what He is. And the same is true of Son and Spirit, in their total giving over of themselves to each other. (In fact, if we read the Bible carefully, we will see that Jesus never spoke of Himself as having any kind of individual identity apart from his Father and Spirit.) The Trinity, then, is love play *par excellence*. These three persons are totally and eternally taken out of themselves to dwell in each other. Their presence to each other is play, not work. It is intimacy, not ministry. They simply exult in each other's goodness, without the least anxiety to add to it or change it in any way.

Such love play is a model for the sexual intimacy of spouses, which is, in turn, a model for the whole of life for all of us. It is the ideal standard that we ought to imitate in all that we do. Students and teachers, priests and parishioners, rulers and subjects, bosses and employees — and most of all, husbands and wives — must be quick to meet each other's needs. But that is always a means to an end. The goal is to get needs met, at least for a time, so that we can play. Love play, not ministry, is the highest form of love. In love play, we are taken out of ourselves into a total self-abandon, we are crazy about each other, and ecstatic in our intimacy. Sex can show us the way to God, even as God shows us the way to sex.

CHAPTER THREE

Sex Is New Identity

Sometimes I wonder if it is possible to be both Catholic and American. I don't mean that loyalty to the Vatican conflicts with my patriotism. I mean, rather, that some of the most important features of our culture seem so contrary to the ideals of love and intimacy. We are an affluent society, for example. Obesity is one of our chief health problems, while at the same time, many people in other parts of the world are starving to death. There is a strong materialistic spirit in our society, too, a consumerism that I find hard to reconcile with love. It seems that our success in life is measured by how much money we make, and how much money we spend. There is more prestige in owning two cars than in having two children. And part of that materialism is a spirit of competition. We are not just expected to devote our lives to earning and spending money. We are to be earners and consumers in competition with each other. An effort to win out over someone else in that kind of competition, to prove oneself superior, goes directly against the loving identification of others as one's other selves. And that identification is necessary for love, necessary for intimacy. Jesus' command that we should be in the world but not of it seems to apply directly to us as we live in twentieth century America.

One of the hardest ways to be in the world but not of it is to try to make sexual intimacy a top priority. Intimacy is not a value for most Americans. We tend to admire rugged individuals, self-made men, those who prove themselves by their independence. But the sexual values of our culture are particularly horrendous. In our contemporary society, sex is something that people "have". And "having sex" means intercourse — casual sexual intercourse, with "no strings attached". Sex is an activity separated from the rest of people's lives, something that they do rather than what they are to each other. Sexual intercourse is a form of entertainment. One of Dustin Hoffman's lines in the popular movie *The Graduate* said it very well. When he was caught in his sexual liaison with Mrs. Robinson, he said to her husband, "What we did didn't mean anything more than a handshake."

Such casual sexual activity is the most popular version of romantic love in today's American culture. It is the theme of all our soap operas, of much of our popular music, of many movies and TV programs. *The Love Boat* and *Three's Company*, two of our most watched programs, hardly ever portray anything else. And the well-liked movie and stage play of a few years ago, *Same Time, Next Year*, was seen as a comic version of love and sex. In that story, a man and woman, each married to someone else, met once a year, for nearly twenty years, for a week-end of secret sex and conversation. Both their talk and their sex were more exciting than what they found in their homes the rest of the time. But their secret meetings were presented in a very positive light, and in fact were meant to be funny. At the end of the story, their true colors were revealed. Their intercourse, exuberant as it was, was selfish on both sides. For when the man's wife died, he asked his yearly partner to leave her husband and marry him. His reason: "I don't want to live alone." Her refusal was just as selfish: "I'm too comfortable in my marriage." No passion there — sexual arousal and release, yes. Exciting conversation, yes. But no affection, no concern for, or devotion to, each other. These two kept their loving concern centered on themselves. They had no intimacy. They were eager for the thrills of intercourse, all right. But they had no urgency for each other, no desire to belong to each other. They used each other, year after year. And that was supposed to be funny!

Such sexual activity is the direct opposite of the love-making of a sacramental couple, of the passion by which they live in each other's minds and hearts in an ecstasy of belonging. And yet, such casual relationships are accepted in our culture. We can't even call them relationships. They are handshakes — episodic encounters in which sexual itches get scratched. Any couple, then, who want real sexual intimacy will have to struggle against the grain of contemporary American culture. We will have be in the world, but not of it.

The problem is not just that love is equated with episodic sexual encounters which don't produce any intimacy. The problem is not just that such casual partners don't care about each other. One of the worst features of our popular culture is its vulgarity. The fixation on casual sexual activity is coarse and sleazy. *Three's Company* was a very popular TV program for almost a decade, and it had two main themes: impotence and homosexuality. Both of these were the object of one vulgar joke after another. And yet, the program had wide appeal. The same sleaziness is evident in our movies, where vulgar displays of nudity and even sexual activity are common in films that are aimed at teenage movie-goers. The lyrics of rock music are notoriously coarse, as is the language of its young fans. Anyone who wants to think of sex as tender, as mysterious and precious, as sacred, will certainly be out of step with much of our society.

Along with this casual and even vulgar view of sex, we have to look at the "rugged individualism" which is so admired in our culture. This view makes intimacy almost impossible. It shows a real fear of becoming attached to someone, of getting trapped and losing one's freedom. A more typical approach to life, especially for American men, is to "hang loose", "stay cool", "don't make any promises to women". In other words, keep your options open, don't get involved. Just try putting sexual intimacy up against this background as an ideal! How can anyone who prizes such a cool, detached independence even consider sexual activity which says, "I am wholly yours," "I am no longer my own person, but yours," "Ask me anything you want — I can't resist you"? The American way is, rather, to say "O.K. for now — but don't count on me to be here when you wake up in the morning. When I leave, don't even ask if I'll be back."

We who want maximum sexual intimacy will also have problems with negative attitudes in our culture about the sense of touch. Our sense of touch is extremely important. It is, in fact, our chief way of knowing that we love and are loved. Even a small but direct contact has an effect on people. For example, students checking books out of a library were questioned by psychologists about how they perceived the library — as a warm and accepting place, where they felt comfortable, or as cold and forbidding. Those who found it warm and comfortable had been touched ever so slightly by the librarians when they checked their books out. The others had not been so touched. Psychologists have also proven, beyond any doubt, that babies who are cuddled and fondled a lot actually develop a greater number of brain cells than those who are left alone in their cribs for long periods of time. But adults need cuddling and hugging, too. The sense of touch gives us a powerful, primitive reassurance about our own goodness and worth, and about the goodness of the world.

One episode of *Hill Street Blues* illustrated this point wonderfully. During the program, Joyce Davenport had discovered that she could not have children, and told her husband so. He had had an especially hard day, too, having been surprised by an armed robber whom he killed on his way home from his job at the Hill Street Police Station. Joyce said, "I still have a lot of motherly instincts, though." To which Frank Furillo, her shaken husband, replied, "I could use a little mothering myself about now." At that point, Joyce folded him into her arms and said, "Come here, Baby." That was one of the sexiest scenes ever shown on American television. It was a moment of the kind of intimacy that is truly sacramental. But it did not set well with the general American public. It was too tender. It made a man weak and dependent on his woman.

The point about culture is very important. We absorb the attitudes and values of our national culture without even realizing it. And many American attitudes simply make sexual intimacy, sex in our sense of the term, impossible. For sex is passion, and passion means an eagerness to belong to someone else. Passion means enthusiasm for the one we love, a feeling that the man or woman we love is truly wonderful in a unique way, unlike anyone else we know. And part of that uniqueness is our beloved's love for us. Once that kind of love becomes mutual, there is a bond, a commitment, which we make with our whole hearts. Passion makes our beloved irresistible. People who love each other with such passion do not value each other in terms of money. They don't try to get and spend money in competition with each other. Psychologists are beginning to see more and more marriages in which the wife earns more money than the husband, and her superiority creates problems for him and for the marriage. Such husbands feel that their virility has been undermined, that they are being robbed of their masculinity. Men in our culture truly are expected to prove their manliness by competitive money-making.

But passion makes such questions totally beside the point. When a couple are crazy in their desire to belong to each other, money is a means to an end. Their intimacy has certain material requirements. They and their children need food, clothing, shelter, medical care, education, entertainment, and so on. There must be a certain income to pay for all of these material needs. But it doesn't occur to intimate spouses to think that their own worth as persons is linked to their ability to get that money. A passionate wife who earns more than her husband certainly does not think that she is superior to him. Nor does he feel that his manhood is threatened by her income. They would never think of drawing up a marital property contract, as a guide to dividing up their resources if they ever were to separate. What is his is hers, and vice versa. People who value intimacy, in fact, don't judge anyone — not themselves, nor each other, not their children, nor anyone else — in terms of money.

Sexual intercourse is different for them, too. Far from being a mere handshake, with no strings attached, love-making is a way of binding intimate spouses to each other more and more tightly, more and more deeply, more and more passionately. It is a promise to "be there" when they wake up in the morning. It is, of course, not just a promise to "be there" in some mere physical sense, but to be there with a certain attitude of mind. When passionate spouses get up in the morning, they look at each other in a special light. Even if they have made love hundreds or thousands of times, each episode generates new passion, new devotion, and a new commitment to each other. They cannot be casual about sex, nor enjoy vulgar jokes, coarse music and conversation, or sleazy TV programs and movies. Unlike the couple in *Same Time, Next Year,* they don't refuse each other favors for selfish reasons. Their very relationship is an ongoing state which says, "Ask me anything you want. I showed you last night how irresistible you are to me. You still are." When such spouses have to be apart for most of their days, they say "goodbye" to each other reluctantly, and can hardly wait to be together again.

Dr. Joyce Brothers, the famous psychologist, shows a good example of such passion. She travels a lot, to all parts of the country, to give lectures. But she tries to minimize her time away from home. For example, if she has a talk on the West Coast on a Monday night, and another one on Thursday morning, she does not stay over, living in a hotel on Tuesday and Wednesday. Many wives, and husbands, too, would think, "Well, since I'm all the way out here, and have to be here again in a couple of days, I might as well stay over. It seems silly to fly all the way back to New York just for two days, and then fly back to California again." Joyce Brothers and her husband do not think that the extra trip is silly. She will give her talk on Monday night, fly back to New York, and then fly back to California again on Wednesday night, just so that she and her husband can be together in the meantime. He has a fine explanation of why he wants her to do that: "Life just doesn't seem real when she isn't around." What makes life real for passionate spouses is one thing, and one thing alone—each other. Being together is their top priority, and it is worth spending a great deal of money that might go for other things instead. To passionate spouses, their intimacy is what makes life real, and each day of it is so precious that they will pay very high prices for it, indeed.

Intimacy, then, is against the ideals of our culture, especially for men. An intimate man is no rugged individualist, doing his own thing, hanging loose and staying cool. He is hot—hot with passion for his woman. He is tied down and tied up, his very being so intertwined with his wife's that he seems not to be himself when they are apart. He doesn't do his own thing. In fact, he doesn't have a thing of his own to do. His very identity is one of belonging and dependence. He is not an individual, rugged or otherwise. His dependence on his woman is complete. She is his other self, even as he is hers.

If we were to put all of this in a single word, we would say that sex as we are speaking of it — the passion, desire, and urgency which constitute the sacrament of matrimony — is an aura. Sacramental couples live constantly in the kind of ecstasy that was so evident when they first fell in love and, later, is renewed when they make love. Now, of course, orgasm is a psychologically unique moment, and falling in love is unlike any other experience. But the ecstasy of these two special times is a promise. Such total self-abandon, their complete belonging to each other, is meant to continue long after those special moments come to an end. A couple who have fallen in love are meant to stay in love all the rest of their life together. Their falling in love should not just be an event of their youth which is soon over as they settle down to a more sober and restrained life together. The ecstasy of intercourse is not meant to be episodic, an oasis of passion that a couple occasionally enjoy as they cross the desert of married life. Of course they cannot spend every moment naked in bed together in a high pitch of emotional excitement. Nor can they have their eyes in contact and their arms intertwined as they go about their daily work and play and association with each other. But their interior state — their attitude toward each other — is meant to be that. Their dwelling in each other's minds and hearts, their enthusiasm for each other, their eager desire to belong to each other and, yes, their desire for the closest possible physical contract — ought to be constants. Sex in that sense should be the aura in which they live, the atmosphere they breathe.

Sex should be to a couple what prayer is to a contemplative religious, or the Eucharist is to a priest. A religious (one who is truly living the religious life, not just going through the motions) does not just say regular prayers. Nor does such a person pray, however deeply, for a few moments, only to emerge from prayer to live like everyone else. No, a true religious tries to make his whole life a life of prayer, to make prayer not just a regular episode but the constant state in which he lives, and moves, and has his being. One of my pastors, when he reads the gospel on Sunday, doesn't really read it. He doesn't look at the book, but at us. He has meditated that gospel so thoroughly that he has it memorized. And his homilies show that he tries to live the gospel as his whole way of life. They are not "talks," not even carefully prepared ones. They are the spontaneous overflow of his own spiritual life. He simply speaks to us out of his faith.

The passion of a sacramental couple must be like that. Their falling in love must be a continuing fall, not just a delicious event of their past which they like to recall, perhaps renew, from time to time. Their falling in love is a beginning, not an end. It is the start of a lifelong process that changes their identities. And as their identities change so do their minds and hearts, their perceptions of each other, their passion for each other.

> Darling, I love you more now than I ever have before. When I first fell for you, I loved you a lot — more than I knew I could. But I love you even more now, after twentyfive years. You have brought out a power to love that I didn't know I had in me. I knew from the start that I loved you with all my heart. But you have made my heart grow, I guess, or something. Because what I felt for you then was very small in comparison to what I feel for you now.

Any husband, and any wife, should be able to speak those words — after a year, five years, ten, twenty-five, or fifty. As long as life lasts, love should grow.

The Irish have a special way of greeting a stranger. They don't say, "Who are you?" or "Where are you from," or "What kind of work do you do?" These are typical American ways of identifying people (especially the last one). Instead, when the Irish meet a new person, they say, "Whose are you?". The question says that our identities are made by the people we belong to. Who we are depends on whose we are. To belong to no one is not an ideal — like the independence of the rugged individual. To belong to no one is a tragedy. It is to *be* no one.

A sacramental couple, then, even after many years of living together, will still belong to each other in passionate desire. They will still be in love. They will belong to each other more than ever before. They will show the same self-abandon that they once fell into without even trying. They will have no more need to prove themselves right, to stand on their own feet, to be independent and autonomous, than they did in the first flush of their romance. Sexual sparks will fly continuously between them, creating an energy field of love.

A passionate home, then, is not like the one in a cartoon some years ago: a teenaged girl, lolling romantically on her bed, asked her mother, in all seriousness, "Mother, were you ever in love?" Many teenagers, perhaps most, find it impossible to picture their parents making love. They know, in some vague way, that they do (or once did), but they have no clear picture in their minds of how it happens. Part of that vagueness is just a lack of sex education, of information about sexual intercourse in general. But many of those who do have the right "book learning" about intercourse also find it hard to picture their parents in the act. And the reason is that they do not see their parents as being particularly passionate people. They see a sort of calm, take-it-for-granted atmosphere between their parents, and find it hard to picture them in a state of real sexual excitement.

Of course we don't mean that children should witness their parents' lovemaking. What we mean is that passion should not be confined to the bedroom. It ought to penetrate and pervade the whole house, all the time. As it is now, we tend to think that a couple who look at each other with hungry eyes, who cannot take their eyes off each other, who can scarcely keep their hands off each other, are either unmarried lovers or else newlyweds. But why should not the glow of romance, the afterglow of intercourse, go on forever? We ought to wonder, indeed, how a couple who have experienced the awesome unity of orgasm can be blasé about each other the next morning, or ever after, at any time.

"I've got you under my skin. I've got you under the hide of me." Passion was more popular when that song was written — at least, passion for lovers. People in love are still expected to be together even when they are apart, to live in each other's minds and hearts. Their whole way of life is romantic, and passion is the air that they breathe. Their sexual desire draws them into total absorption with each other. But for some strange reason, we assume that marriage is the death of such romance. We advise young people to "settle down and get married", the implication being that excitement and romance are for the immature. We tell young couples to enjoy the thrill of romance because "it won't last". Married life is seen as the end of passion and the beginning of "more serious" matters — meaning a dull, unexciting routine. Desire for each other is expected to die. Earning a living, keeping house, raising children all take priority over passion. And so, passion cools. And as passion cools, lovers become friends, partners, roommates, instead.

The overall atmosphere in which such spouses live reflects a decline in their sexual activity, too — a decline in frequency as well as in quality. In fact, spouses often do what most of us do in other relationships with people. When we meet someone new, we are wary and somewhat reserved in our conversation. We "feel each other out" verbally, raising certain subjects and voicing certain opinions carefully, so that we gradually discover what is "safe" and what is not. It is typical of many friendships and partnerships, such as roommates in college, or office mates, to discover a "safe" area in which to talk to each other, and then respect the boundaries of that area very carefully. And then the people involved get along quite well. They never fight. Their relationship is peaceful, pleasant, satisfying for both. But it is also dead, or at least stagnant. Such relationships cannot grow, because the boundaries worked out by mutual agreement prevent any new intimacy.

Tragically, many couples do the same. They assume that love is for the young and the immature, and that after they are married, they must get "serious." Romance quickly fades. Two people who originally found each other irresistible, and wanted to think of nothing else all day long, decide that fulfilling certain roles is more important. Their fond gestures and looks, their tender tone of voice, their frequent passionate touches, all become things of the past. Their attention shifts, away from each other and toward their "duties and obligations". Their passion cools. They begin to live like brother and sister, except for occasional passionate interludes on special occasions. They are congenial enough, considerate of each other, pleasant. And they meet now and then for sexual arousal and intercourse. But that, too, falls into a certain mechanical routine and — incredible as it may seem — loses its excitement. Their passion becomes dormant. And with it, their sacrament becomes dormant, too.

Remember what we said earlier about sex being a powerful sacrament because of its dramatic clarity? The passion of couples ought to grow, not decline as as they take up their life together. Married couples ought to be more obviously in love than anyone else. Their passion should increase, and grow in visibility, all the days of their lives. What would we think of a priest who thought that Holy Orders was the ordination ceremony? With that idea in mind, he would see his ordination as the end of a search, not as the beginning of a new life. Once the ordination and reception were over, he could come down out of the clouds and "get serious". What would we think of a man who said, the day after his first mass, "Well, now I can get back to normal life. I start my job at the bank tomorrow." He would not really be a priest at all. Priests are expected to begin, and then to continue, a new life once they are ordained, not go back to their old, lay life. The reason a man is expected to do priestly work is that he has assumed a new identity. Ordination is the death of his old self and the beginning of a new life, a new identity, a new role in the community of intimates that is the Church. He is, more importantly, to begin to love in a new way. And his new love creates new communion, new intimacy, with his people.

A couple who fall in love, marry, and then "settle down" to a "more mature love", one that is cool and dispassionate, make the same mistake as a priest who would go through his ordination ceremony and then go on to live the life of a layman. They would have mistaken their wedding for the sacrament of matrimony. And that sacrament would be, to them, the end of a quest rather than the beginning of a new life. Having wooed and won each other, they would feel free to "get back to normal", to pick up again the single identities that they had before they fell in love.

Such a cooling of passion is tragic, indeed. Couples are not meant to be "normal", any more than priests are. Their vocation is not to have a wedding. It is to live a new life, with new identities, all their life long, in everything they say and do, every moment of every day. And that new life is sex, the passionate devotion and desire which bind them together in total belonging. True, the wedding is over and done with in a short time — as a ceremony. But that ceremony recognizes, celebrates, and licenses their being in love. That being in love is their sacrament.

The idea that a couple must remain in love — must, in fact, deliberately cultivate their passion so that it will grow to the utmost, as the focus of their life together — seems startling at first. Couples who have good communication, who are affectionate and kind to each other, and who generate sexual sparks when they come together for lovemaking, are usually considered to have good marriages. Well, such marriages may be good in some sense — in the sense of a secular contract, perhaps. But they are not good in a sacramental sense. They are, in fact, tragic. So two people live together peaceably, don't fight, don't even consider breaking up, but let their passion become episodic. So what? Even the pagans do that. What is sacramental about matrimony is sex — the desire, passion, urgency that draws people out of their separate identities to belong totally to each other. Sacramental couples are those who image forth, in a clear and dramatic way, the ecstatic life — not just ecstatic episodes, but ecstatic life — that resembles the inner life of the three divine persons. Passion is what the sacrament of matrimony is all about.

St. Paul speaks quite eloquently and clearly about the kind of passionate belonging to each other that should typify Catholic couples. If we ponder his words a bit, we can see that it is not too strong to call marriage a change in the personal identities of the spouses. They are no longer the persons that they once were, because of their belonging to each other. St. Paul's words are stark:

> The husband should fulfill his conjugal obligations toward his wife, the wife hers toward her husband. A wife does not belong to herself, but to her husband; equally, a husband does not belong to himself, but to his wife. Do not deprive one another, unless perhaps by mutual consent for a time, to devote yourselves to prayer. (I Cor. 7, 3-5. New American Bible).

St. Paul is writing to his converts in Corinth, who were pagan Greeks before they became Christians. And he is answering some questions that they had written to him. In their society, sexual promiscuity was quite widely accepted. And some of the religion around them regarded sexual intercourse as an evil action, even for married people. In fact, they also considered marriage evil, for that reason. In the passage from which we have taken the words above, St. Paul first reassures the Corinthians that sex is not evil, and that marriage is good for Christians. Then he answers a question as to whether spouses can refuse each other sexual relations in order to prepare for, and take part in, various religious rites. (It seems that night is the best time for sex as well as for prayer). Paul affirms that husband and wife have certain obligations to each other, and that they cannot refuse sexual intercourse to each other. They may refrain from sexual activity for religious reasons, but only by mutual consent, and only for a short time.

But what we must notice is Paul's reason for these answers. It is not a vision of marriage as a contract, a legal agreement by which both parties assume certain rights and duties. No, Paul's reason is deeper and more personal than that, and it marks the difference between pagan (or secular) and sacramental marriages: in a Christian marriage, husband and wife belong to each other. They no longer belong to themselves, but only to each other. A husband no longer has any say over what he will and will not do, and when. He is not his own person any more. He is given over to his wife, and belongs to her. And the same is true of her. Notice the equality between spouses. A woman, too, has no say any more as to whether her body will be available to her husband, and when, and how. She is no longer her own person. She belongs to him.

Such belonging comes about through identification that we mentioned earlier. Each person, in a loving relationship, takes the other as his other self. Hence, a husband no longer has, or is, the self that he once was. His wife is his self, and he is hers. Their very identities—who they are as persons—have changed. They can no longer distinguish themselves from each other. Whatever a husband does for his wife, he is doing for himself. Whatever he would do for himself, must be something that he does for his wife. And her belonging to him is just as complete. She can no longer even think of herself apart from her identification with him, for he is her very self. Paul makes this identity even more clear in another place: "Husbands should love their wives as they do their own bodies. He who loves his wife loves himself." (Eph. 5: 28, New American Bible).

Paul's words to the Corinthians refer specifically to sexual intercourse, to spouses being available to each other for that particular action. That is what his Greek converts had asked about. But of course he is not referring to that action in its mere physical aspect. He refers to the relationship between the spouses, their belonging to each other as the context of their sexual activity. The fact that prayer and lovemaking can conflict with each other is a clear sign that one is as much a part of married life, of what husband and wife owe to each other, as is the other.

And so, husbands belong to their wives all day and all night, every day and every night. They are to be totally available to their wives, for whatever those wifely selves of theirs may need — conversation, breadwinning, housework, recreation, and sex. Husbands belong to their wives completely. And wives are to be totally, constantly available to the husbands who are their new selves as well. A wife cannot refuse her husband intercourse, but she can't refuse him anything else, either. She belongs to him. He owns her. She is his very self, even as he is hers.

Such belonging of one person to another, such devotion and availability, are astonishing, indeed. How can St. Paul recommend such a thing? He can because of one simple reality that is at the heart of the marital symbol: passion. Passion, and passion alone, enables people to belong to each other with such completeness. In fact, passion urges them to such belonging. Passion makes them irresistible to each other, so that, when they are in that passionate state, they cannot help giving themselves over to each other completely. Don't lovers say, in words, in songs, in countless little actions, "Take me — I'm all yours"? Doesn't sexual intercourse say, with a special drama and clarity, "Let me pour myself out for you! I want to hold back nothing of myself"? But those two special ways of showing self-abandon, or enthusiasm to belong to each other, are not meant to be isolated episodes. The passion of urgent self-abandon, the desire for total belonging to each other — sex, in a word — is meant to be constant. It defines the identities and the relationship of the two people involved. It follows, then, that if a couple allow their passion to become episodic, they are allowing their sacrament to become episodic. Whenever passion cools, they revert to their former, unmarried identities.

Does a husband want intercourse before breakfast, at a time when his busy spouse hasn't planned it? Then there should be no question, no question whatsoever, as to her consent. Consent, indeed! She will respond to his advances with her wholehearted passion. And that response is not even a decision. She will not even think about whether or not she will join in. Her urgency then is nothing more than a continued living out of a gift she made long ago — the gift of her entire self. If she were to make a decision, to stop and think, "Now, will I or won't I?", she would be acting as if she still had a self to give. But she does not. She has no option, no way to wonder, even for a moment, whether she will consent or not. She will not even think in terms of an obligation, of what she owes her beloved mate, of duty and rights. Even an act of generous, benevolent compliance might imply some remnant of self-control and self-possession. But no, she will live those clear words of St. Paul's: she does not belong to herself, but to her husband. Her love for herself is her love for him, because he is her very self. She responds with the passion that is always there for him.

To take a similar example, does she want intimate conversation, a revelation of his feelings about his work, say, or about their relationship? Does she spring this request on him as a surprise, something he hadn't counted on when he planned his day? Well, if they are passionate spouses, he will not have planned "his" day. His days are not his to plan — they are his wife's. Hence, there will be no question about his responding to her desire to talk. Of course he will. Hasn't he long since given his entire self to her, including his innermost feelings and ability to verbalize them? He doesn't even have a decision to make. It is not a question of whether or not he will humor her, going along in order to get along. He will not talk to her as an act of generosity, after a decision to comply. He has no decision to make, no self to make decisions about. Such calculations are for someone who still has, and controls, a private self. But a passionate husband does not. His wife is himself. Her needs are his needs. His love for himself is a love for her as his other self. His passion will speak to her at once.

What St. Paul means, then, when he tells the Corinthians that a spouse may not refuse sexual activity when it is desired, is that such a spouse would be denying his or her marital identity. The refusal of intercourse, and of the total availability that intercourse epitomizes, is wrong even when done for what looks like a religious motive. Prayer and other devotions, even preparation for these, cannot take priority over intimacy for sacramental spouses. In fact, sex — as their ongoing intimacy — is the foundation of their prayer and other religious exercises. Hence, it would make no sense at all to disrupt that intimacy for the sake of prayer. Any praying done under those circumstances would not have its marital quality. Conjugal obligations, then, the obligations toward intercourse as well as conversation, are not matters of justice so much as matters of intimacy. Are we going to live sacramentally or not? If we are, we are going to live in passionate self-abandon, all day, every day, and nothing else will ever take priority over that. Without that, we simply are not the persons we claim to be, the persons we became when we fell in love and made love: each other's very selves.

There is nothing wrong with loving each other as brother and sister. In fact, that is what all Christians are supposed to do. "See how these Christians love one another." "By this will all men know that you are my disciples, that you love one another." But when spouses love each other in that way, something is seriously wrong. They have, in a sense, abandoned each other. They have fallen back into their original, single identities. They have become unfaithful to each other. Fidelity does not just mean confining sexual activity to one's legal partner. It is much deeper than that. It is living out the giving over of one's entire self to the beloved in passion. Dispassionate couples, those who have allowed their ardor to cool, may be fine practicing Catholics. They may be good companions and kind helpers to each other. They may share a lot of secrets and common interests. They may have several well loved children. Such spouses are close to each other in many ways. But they have no distinctively marital intimacy. They live in brotherly love.

Intimacy means belonging to each other totally. And nothing but passion can create that kind of belonging. People who withhold their passion from each other withhold an important part of themselves. In fact, when spouses do that, they withhold the most important part of all. And holding part of ourselves back creates distance, not intimacy. There is simply no way in which dispassionate couples can be sacramental. People who are their own persons, in control, self-possessed, cannot symbolize a God of three persons who are totally, passionately, ecstatically poured forth to each other.

Maybe it sounds harsh, but it is true nonetheless: couples who allow their passion to cool come very close to practicing the kind of casual sex that is typical of our secular culture. There is an important difference, of course. Couples with good, stable but dispassionate marriages are better off than those who engage in one night stands, in premarital sex, extra-marital sex, and so on. In their devotion to, and affection for each other, they have a bond that builds a true intimacy. Dispassionate spouses often do live in love, and that is what counts most basically for all Christians. Those whose sexual lives are entirely casual do not care about anyone except themselves, and thus do not have even that kind of loving intimacy. . . .Their actions, which speak louder than words, say, "I'm all yours for now because that suits the sexual desire that I happen to feel at this moment. But when it passes, I'll be my own person again—until next time. Of course, there may not be any next time. Don't count on it."

And yet, couples whose desire has faded are similar to such casual couples in one important way: their passion is episodic, and then their marital intimacy is, too. The intimacy they have is fraternal, not marital. It is good and even holy. But it is not the sacrament of matrimony. Sacramental intimacy has to be passionate. It has to shout to people, in a voice so loud and clear that they cannot ignore it, that life and salvation are ecstatic, that what saves us is our enthusiastic, utter, exciting abandoning of ourselves to each other. Both casual couples and dispassionate married ones trivialize the power of sex. They hold it in check, so that it does not change their very identities. They withhold it from other people, so that it does not become evident to them. And they inhibit its growth. For both kinds of couples, sex is reduced to an activity, rather than being a state in which they live. Their passion, and thus their belonging to each other, become episodic. Sex, then, is not their life. It is something to do together, a way to release tension, a time for putting problems aside and healing loneliness. In those moments, each seeks his own momentary feelings of warmth and closeness.

All of these benefits are important, of course. Casual sex wouldn't be so popular if it didn't do something for people. But it does not touch the most important concern of every human being who lives even one inch below the surface of life: how am I to learn to love and be loved, to trust and be trustworthy, to belong? How am I to find credible the reality of the God Who is Love? Great simultaneous orgasms three times a week, right on schedule, are not enough. Even the pagans do that. What we need is some convincing evidence that a whole life of loving and being loved is possible. And if married couples don't give us that evidence, who will?

Passion that is reduced to mere arousal for intercourse, then, is not sacramental. Episodic passion can only produce episodic affection and devotion. And if we stop to think about it, episodic devotion is no devotion at all. To say, whether in words or in actions, "I'm all yours for the moment, but don't count on anything when this is over" is the same as saying "I'm not really yours even for this moment. I am my own self, and my own self I intend to remain." The decline of sexual desire in a marriage, then, is no small matter. It is truly tragic. It leads a couple not to any intimate communion, but to living two separate lives in the same house. But the Good News — the message that is supposed to draw people to the Church by the thousands — is not that sex is O.K., that sex is permissible to those who have gone through a certain ceremony. The Good News is not even that sex is a natural human good that can be elevated to the supernatural order if we engage in it with pure motives. The Good News is that sex is holy, that human love play is one way in which we can take part in the love play of the Trinity. To make it anything less is to cheapen it, indeed.

Passionate spouses live *in* each other rather than *with* each other. Instead of doing things together, they are together, even when they are apart. They live in each other's minds and hearts, thoughts and affections. Their passion is their communion with God. When spouses perceive each other correctly, through the prism of sexual desire, they contemplate God as well. And passion is their spirituality, not a distraction from it. In fact, intimacy is the spirituality of a couple. We don't call it spiritual because it is somehow not material, not a part of the physical world. There is nothing more material than sex, which is the most intense use of our sense of touch. There is no greater physical closeness than that of an intimate couple. But that physical intimacy is a life in which the two bring their entire selves under the domination of the Holy Spirit. Our spiritual life is our life in the Spirit. For couples, life in the Spirit is passion. Without passion, they have no life at all as a couple.

CHAPTER FOUR

Sex Is Dying and Rising

'Tinkering in the garage again all evening? O.K., Buster. But try loving me up at bedtime and see what you get. You seem to think I'm like one of your tools, lying around waiting for you to use me and then set me aside without a thought until next time. Well, that's a game two can play.'

Sarah was talking to herself, not to anyone else. But she meant what she said. Something had happened between her and Richard since they were first married. A pattern of manipulative game playing had somehow become established between them. It wasn't always like that. When they were courting, the two of them tingled with desire every minute they were together. And when they had to part for a day or so, they could hardly wait to get together again, to feast their hungry eyes and hungry hands on each other.

Sarah was aware that something was wrong, though she didn't know what it was. She realized that her pattern of doling out her sexual favors to Richard as a reward for his good behavior was a far cry from the excitement that she used to feel. Richard's advances used to mean instant excitement. Now she found herself saying "No" more and more often. It was a little like the control she used to exercise when they were dating, and her aroused fiancé would urge her to "go all the way". But that was different. Then her heart felt like saying "Yes", and Richard knew that she hated saying "No" because she was as passionately aroused as he. Then he would agree with her, and both of them would put the brakes on their feelings. But they did so with real regret, looking forward to the time when their passion could be set free.

Then the day came when their passion was set free. The wild abandon of their honeymoon lasted for months, years, even. But gradually a subtle change set in. Dick and Sarah found a comfortable, dependable way of making love, and settled into that routine. They settled into comfortable routines in many other areas of their life, too, as they gradually negotiated one practical decision after another. Dick really enjoyed his work, and became more and more absorbed in it. Sarah found that many times when she had been looking forward to a good evening's conversation about their love, their romantic memories and hopes for the future, Dick would have work to do or be too tired. She couldn't remember when he had last called her from work to say, "I love you." And Sarah, too, had found her domain as she took charge of the household. As the children began to arrive, her mind and heart were filled more and more with them. She found herself too tired for lovemaking at bedtime, and too preoccupied in the evening and morning. But tonight she was worried. For it seemed to her that she and Dick had not just settled down — they were beginning to settle *for* what they had settled down to. They didn't enjoy each other as much as they used to. Both sex and conversation had lost their former zip.

Dick had his worries, too. When he came home from work that evening, he had loving on his mind. He greeted his wife with an extra lusty kiss, and an extra little squeeze — signals that she had long ago learned to recognize. But instead of giving him a passionate kiss in return, and writhing with delight at his squeeze, she stiffened a bit, pulled away, and said, "You wouldn't believe what a day I had today! When I get to bed, I'm going to go right to sleep." Dick said, "O.K. I plan to work on the car a bit, and then go to sleep myself." But what he said to himself was, "I'll be darned if I'm going to beg, like a little puppy dog. I don't need you and I'll prove it. Just watch me!"

Dick and Sarah are a very typical couple with a good marriage which could become better. It could be luminously sacramental if the two of them would change. Their marriage is a lasting, stable relationship without any major emotional problems that would call for professional counseling. These two spouses are still in love and living together happily. Despite the decline in their passion, they feel content with their marriage. They have found other satisfactions, and their days go by rather smoothly, without major battles that would threaten to break them apart. Their children are happy and well-adjusted, doing well in school and getting along with their friends. But Dick and Sarah have heard the call to something much higher than a "good" marriage. They are called to a dying and a rising to new life that is beyond the wildest dreams of either. The game they are playing is one very common way in which married couples act out the sin of Adam. They are living in a kind of shame that blocks their passionate intimacy. That game can be healed, though, by the grace of their sacrament. Let's see how that healing might take place.

One lovely summer evening a whole group of such couples got together to celebrate their good marriages. But the conversation took a surprising turn. One of the men, a trusted adviser to the group, announced, "I'd like to address the #1 problem in good marriages, the 'No-Power' that women use to control the sexual relationship." The women groaned. It seemed like he was out to get them, as usual. Why was it always the wives that were at fault? Why was the conversation always about how they needed to change? The real problem in their minds was their husbands' playing "Silent Sam," refusing to reveal their feelings in intimate conversation. That was what controlled their intimacy and kept the fires of passion at a low ebb. It's hard to warm up to someone who uses sex as a way of avoiding conversation. Yet they felt that they were being accused of using conversation to avoid sex. And the husbands in the group seemed to agree.

But their adviser persisted. "Isn't it true," he asked, "that the wife usually determines the When, the Where, and even the Whether of a couple's lovemaking?" Gradually the women in the group came to see that he was right, that the kind of manipulative game that Dick and Sarah had settled into was common in their marriages. Several hours of painful but revealing dialogue followed, and that dialogue brought to light in a new way the real death — the death to self — that marital holiness calls for. The women had simply assumed, without even knowing that they were doing so, a control over the level of passion in their marriages. And that control extended over the whole relationship between themselves and their husbands. They not only said "Yes" or "No" to their husbands' sexual advances, setting the time, place, and mood. They also set the thermostat for passion, making love sometimes with reluctance, sometimes with a dutiful restraint, at other times even with a coolness that showed that their minds were really on something else. Not that they fantasized other lovers. They just let their attention wander to the next day's grocery list, or the children's dental appointments. Some of the more honest ones had to laugh as they admitted that sometimes, in the midst of the most tender, intimate activity that human beings are capable of, they would be saying to themselves, "Come on, let's get this over with. I've got lots to do tomorrow." Others would say, in their minds, "You're not going to get my body until after we talk. We're not friends right now." They made conversation a precondition for sex.

The situation is not simple, of course, for husbands play along with the game and exercise their kind of control, too. Sometimes they are also glad to avoid intimacy and glad to blame it on their wives. For when a man does not open up and share his feelings with his wife, he is controlling her, and controlling the level of their passion and the depth of their intimacy, just as effectively as she does with her "No-Power". When a man is obviously upset about something, and his wife asks, "What's the matter?", his curt "Nothing", or "I don't want to talk about it" puts a wall between them that is just as solid as the one she constructs by tightening up to resist his amorous squeezes. There are benefits to both spouses in finding ways to avoid intimacy. And there are subtle benefits for both in letting the other person build the walls. That way, they can respect the walls and put the blame on each other. Intimacy is scary, and the human heart is devious beyond words in finding ways to avoid it. Many of those ways are not fully conscious. Some are not even conscious at all. Many of them come to us through our culture. We act them out because we make certain assumptions about what it is to be a man, and what it is to be a woman. We may go for years without questioning those assumptions, or even becoming aware of them. The years go by because we find our cautious, inhibited patterns comfortable. They allow us to avoid the pain of becoming vulnerable.

Our culture, which affects all of us very deeply, reinforces the tendency to avoid intimacy that all of us are born with. We can see inhibitions, some intimacy-avoidance games, in any relationship that lasts for any length of time and achieves any depth at all. When we meet new people, we just naturally "feel each other out" in conversation. We sort out which topics we can talk about without getting into painful disagreements, and which ones we had better avoid if we don't want some hurt feelings, perhaps even a breakup. Once we find these "safe" topics, we cling to them and avoid others, thus settling into a comfortable routine. We can associate with each other and enjoy each other for years, without facing any of those painful issues.

In marriages, however, the stakes are much higher. The breakup of a marriage is more painful than the breakup of other relationships, especially for those who get married with high ideals for themselves. And conflicts with a spouse are more painful than conflicts with a friend or a business partner. The reason why is passion. Passion is at the center of marriages. Sexual conflicts are more painful and more frightening than others. Sexual rejections are more painful and more frightening than others. Sexual intimacy is the most frightening kind of intimacy. But its rewards are also the greatest of rewards, worth the risk, the pain, the vulnerability.

The reason why sexual vulnerability is so great, and sexual intimacy so thrilling, is that sexuality is central to what we are as persons. When

I succeed as a man or a woman, I succeed as a person. And that is a total success. Other failures don't matter. But when I fail, or am rejected, as a man or a woman, I fail, or am rejected, as a person. And that is a total failure, making other successes unimportant. For *man* or *woman* is the kind of person that I am, basic to everything I do. It should not be surprising, then, that we find ways of avoiding sexual vulnerability, which reaches its high point in lovemaking. What Sarah and Richard are trying to do, without recognizing the fact, is to protect themselves against sexual hurts and rejections. Richard controls the level of passion in their verbal communication because he then feels safe from the hurtful things that Sarah might say to him. He protects his masculinity that way. For if she knows his feelings, she knows many ways in which to ridicule him, to insult him, to reject him, to ignore him. And Sarah controls the conditions of their lovemaking in order to feel safe as a woman. If she allows passion free rein, if she gives up her power to say "No" and thus her control over Richard's behavior toward her, she leaves herself open to the possibility of being used, of becoming the object of a selfish, bestial passion. She risks becoming a thing instead of a person, a sex object.

With these possibilities for sexual hurts, it is no wonder that our culture has invented ways for people to guard against them. One of its most powerful ways is the stereotypes, the false patterns held up as ideals, which teach little girls what it is to be a woman, and little boys what it is to be a man. We can see those stereotypes at work in Richard and Sarah's marriage. And we can see how men who withhold their verbal intimacy and women who control a couple's sexual activity have to change in order to become more luminously sacramental. The change is nothing less than a death to self, just like the death that Jesus experienced when He went to His crucifixion, begging His Father that the cup of suffering might pass from Him. But that death is also a rising to new life, a life just as glorious as what Jesus awoke to on the third day, in fulfillment of the Scriptures. Building such a sacramental marriage calls for some deep changes, changes in self-awareness first, and then in sharing that awareness. It calls for a hard, critical look at the values of a sinful, secular culture in order to act against them. Rejecting those false sexual values is one way in which sacramental couples obey the command to be "in the world but not of it". Changed awareness leads to changed behavior. And changed behavior leads to new, risen life.

The stereotypes center around the relationships between verbal and sexual intimacy, between sex and conversation in married life. But both words and actions are ways of expressing passion and communicating sexual feelings. Generally, people see verbal intimacy as something that women need and enjoy, and sexual intimacy as a "man's game". Men and women are almost expected to speak two different languages, intercourse (for men) and conversation (for women). Girls are encouraged from their earliest days to talk out their feelings. When we grow up, we have learned to get rid of bad feelings by sharing them with a sympathetic listener. Women usually have several other women that they enjoy such verbal intimacy with — mothers, sisters, friends, coworkers. Men, on the other hand, are expected to be "rugged individuals", to keep their feelings to themselves. In fact there are certain feelings that men are not even supposed to have — the feelings associated with vulnerability. A man is never supposed to feel weak or lonely, frightened or uncertain. He is not supposed to feel a need for closeness and comfort. He is not supposed to want to be cherished as a special person. If he does feel that way, he must not admit it, especially to a woman. He must always be "on top", in charge, strong and invulnerable, especially to his wife. To appear weak or doubtful, lonely or frightened, is to fail as a man. And to fail as a man is to fail as a person.

There is one feeling, however, that a man is allowed to have, to express openly, even to brag about. In fact, men who do not have this feeling must pretend that they do in order to fulfill the stereotype of masculinity. That feeling is best named by the slang term "horny". Men are really considered to be men, to belong, to be "one of the boys" when they brag of having strong sexual appetites. These feelings are not the tender passion of which intimacy is made, but rather bestial, selfish, pleasure-seeking desires for a mechanical and impersonal kind of sexual arousal and release. As I was taught by one of my college professors, once a man gets an erection he must either ejaculate or go crazy. And men (especially those of the age of my fellow students) get erections at the slightest stimulation — the sight of a girl in a strapless evening gown, for example. (The lesson to us girls was to wear straps at least an inch wide, lest we arouse our prom partners to the point of no return.) And that desire has nothing to do with love. It can be satisfied by any available woman.

Women, on the other hand, were — until recently — expected not to have strong sexual feelings or needs, not to enjoy sexual pleasure as intensely or as often as men do. It was our role to "stay cool", to be "nice", to say "No' to the hungry beast with uncontrollable desires who pressed us to "go all the way". More recently, our culture has given women permission to enjoy sex, even to have multiple orgasms. Indeed, in many circles, a man's prowess is no longer measured by his own "horniness". His success depends on his ability to arouse and satisfy his woman. But she still keeps her control — "Not now, Honey. Wait until my mother goes home," or, "Oh, please—I just got my hair fixed." Women's passion may not be under wraps as it was in the recent past; but instead of that newly liberated passion being an ecstatic abandonment to intimacy, it is the reward we dole out for good behavior, especially the right verbal behavior. When we think we've talked enough, we're ready for sex. And so, women's passion, even when liberated, is a tool for control rather than intimacy.

Sometimes the results are downright funny, as men and women accept these stereotypes, first about themselves, and then about each other. Dick, for example, knows that Sarah would like him to talk to her more than he does, especially about his own feelings. But he sees that need as part of a woman's mysterious nature, not realizing that he needs verbal intimacy as much as she does. And so he goes along with it at times, just to humor her—perhaps on a special occasion, like an anniversary. But he doesn't connect such conversation with the overall quality of their relationship. He does not connect it with Sarah's ability to respond to his sexual advances (or make advances of her own). And so, he lives by such proverbs as, "Stick it in her ear," and complains to his friends that "An hour's conversation is the price of my ticket of admission."

Just as Dick occasionally reveals his feelings to Sarah as a favor to her, even though his heart isn't in it, she consents to sexual intercourse, but in a dispassionate, dutiful way, because "that's the way men are". But she keeps her control of the relationship, just as he keeps his. Dick never allows Sarah total freedom to explore his psyche at will. And Sarah never allows him total freedom to enjoy her passionate self-abandon on his terms rather than hers. The two are locked into an intricate, and sometimes ridiculous, psychological dance, each circling warily around the other, approaching more closely and then quickly withdrawing to a safe distance.

What isn't funny, though, is the loneliness that comes from such patterns of intimacy avoidance. Dick is playing the Silent Sam role because that is what is expected of him in the culture in which he was raised. Being taciturn and withdrawn, keeping his feelings to himself, is part of his deepest assumptions about what it is to be a man. But by being Silent Sam, he keeps Sarah from carrying him in her heart. He keeps their intimacy at a low level. After all, we have something—anything—in our minds and hearts by knowing what that something is. And so, when Dick doesn't let Sarah know of his fears and doubts, his loneliness and need for tenderness, he prevents her intimacy with him. After a while, the only satisfaction he gets out of sexual intercourse is a sort of mechanical release of tension. He gets no intimacy with Sarah, no exchange of tender vulnerabilities. He feels a deep, gnawing loneliness.

Sarah, too, feels a deep, gnawing loneliness that she can't even identify clearly for herself. She feels that Dick is being dishonest with her, pretending not to have the feelings that he has. She fears that his dishonesty is somehow rooted in mistrust, that he doesn't trust her enough to become vulnerable to her. She begins to wonder what she must do to win his trust, whether there is something wrong with her as a woman that her man doesn't trust her. And then she feels utterly worthless, and deeply lonely, despite the other intimacies she may enjoy with other people in her life. "If Dick doesn't believe in my love, doesn't trust me enough to talk to me, nothing else matters very much. Maybe I shouldn't have gotten married." The two then begin to reinforce each other's loneliness.

One day Sarah found the courage to tell Dick about these feelings:

> I don't think you've been honest with me. You seem to be half-hearted or reluctant in any kind of personal conversation. You say, 'Gee, Sarah, I think you're wonderful.' And I like to hear that. But I also want to hear some other things that I don't hear, like what gives you sexual pleasure and what doesn't, whether our lovemaking was good for you — you know, sharing yourself with me. If I'm taking bad feelings away from you when we make love, I'd like to know what they are. But, instead, you leave me in the dark.

Sarah's anguish is obvious — she is frustrated and lonely, hungry for better verbal communication. She is asking Dick for his total vulnerability, asking him to risk coming even more fully under her control than he already is. We can see why he might shun that kind of conversation. It would mean giving her the option of hurting him where it hurts the most, in his sense of being a man. But if he doesn't give her that option, if he doesn't reveal to her, in words, his deepest feelings, then he is controlling her. And with any kind of control, intimacy suffers. We can't have intimacy without trust. And trust means giving the other person the chance to control us, in the confident belief that they won't.

Dick was really surprised to hear how Sarah felt about his silence. In his mind, he was just doing what a man is supposed to do. He was being the strong, invulnerable, protective leader. In his mind, his inhibitions about talking out his feelings were a form of tender concern for the wife that he truly cherished. He did not think he was being dishonest, or failing to trust her. As a man, he doesn't find his bad feelings relieved by talking them out with his woman. He feels worse after such conversations. Besides feeling weak and unmanly, he hates himself for burdening Sarah with his troubles. He feels selfish when he lays his fears and anxieties on a fragile, beloved wife whom he wishes to protect and comfort.

And so, when he hears that Sarah feels rejected and lonely when he plays Silent Sam, he feels worse than ever. He feels that he has played to the hilt the role of the male animal as selfish beast.

Human feelings can be just that complex. When Dick verbalizes his feelings, he feels that he has failed to be a man, failed to be strong and protective. At the same time, he feels that he has been a man, in the worst sense of that term, a selfish, uncaring beast. And those feelings carry over into his sexual behavior. He becomes more Silent Sam than ever when he makes love. And then Sarah feels even more lonely and rejected. Sex reinforces their loneliness instead of cementing their intimacy. For Dick, the body language of tender passion, the only such language he knows, turns into an instrument of hurt and loneliness.

The other side of the story is just as complex. It, too, has its funny side and its sadness. For Dick feels Sarah's sexual restraint in several different ways. His view of her "No-Power" is quite different from hers. She would be as surprised to hear his version of her control game as he is to hear what she thinks of his silence. After all, there was a time when she found him completely irresistible. His touch on her arm, his voice on the telephone, was enough to start her juices flowing. She used to hate to say "No" to him. Now she does it quite easily. She may not say it in words. Turning on the Johnny Carson show may be enough, or setting up the ironing board at midnight. She has many nonverbal ways of giving him the message that he needn't even ask. And those little "No" signals are devastating to him. Her turning into a cool, calm and collected housekeeper, a roommate who has other priorities on her agenda, tells him that he is no longer desired as a man. He is no longer desired as a person. He is merely one item on her agenda. When she does comply with his advances, she makes love in a distracted, dispassionate way. Then he is left again with a profound loneliness. He may ejaculate regularly, but his lovemaking as the expression of his own tenderness is rejected. And his own need to be cherished and comforted is deeply frustrated.

One day Dick found the courage to describe his loneliness:

> I feel resentful living in Sarah's house, and I shouldn't. I walk around trying to live in her environment, and thinking that's the way I'm supposed to live. I look for her permission to love her. But I express my masculinity in making love to her. That's the language in which I express my love to her. So, if I allow her to dictate the terms on which I can do that, I allow her to deprive me of my masculinity. It is not just how often, but even how we do it. If the atmosphere

is right on her terms, then she says 'Yes'. But if it isn't, then she says 'No'. But that is devastating to me. I feel angry—on the surface. What I feel underneath the anger is loneliness.

Sarah was, of course, surprised to hear how Dick felt about her "No-Power". In her mind she was just doing what a woman is supposed to do, according to the values and stereotypes of our culture. She had been taught to make verbal intimacy a condition for sexual intimacy, and to take responsibility for curbing the bestial passion that men cannot control. But there is something else, something deep inside Sarah that reinforces that cultural value. She has what all of us have, a deep desire to "keep a piece of myself for myself". Sarah has the same problem we all have, the shame or self-primacy that is symbolized in the sin of Adam. When Dick asks her to give up her "No-Power", he is asking her to become vulnerable, indeed. He is asking her to give up her life for him, to risk coming even more completely under his control than she already is. He is asking her to abandon herself completely to passion, to his passion and hers. And in order to do that, she must trust that his passion is not the appetite for pleasure of a selfish beast, but instead the delicate language of a tender intimacy. Sarah must make an act of faith like the one Jesus made when He went to His death. He had to die in trust, not knowing that He would come out the other side into new and fuller life.

Just as Dick has to give Sarah the option of hurting him, by giving up the control he uses in playing Silent Sam, so must Sarah give Dick the option of hurting her by joining him in passionate sexual abandon. She has to give up her demand for verbal intimacy, and thus risk not having it. But she takes that risk because she believes in Dick's love, in his desire to be verbally close to her, too. On the deepest level, the same law works for both of them, though in different ways. The only way that anyone can avoid vulnerability to another person, the only way we can avoid the risk of being hurt, is to exercise some sort of control over that person. Men often exercise their control by failing to verbalize their feelings. Women exercise theirs by controlling the sexual thermostat. And these two control games become intertwined and reinforce each other in many complicated ways. But control is the basic issue. And control is deadly to intimacy.

Intimacy, however, is what sacramental life is all about. The kind of sexual intimacy that makes a marriage sacramental is scary. It truly means giving up every last shred of our private selves, of those selves that we hug to ourselves. It means confronting the fear that if we let go of ourselves, we will have nothing left. For when we play control games, we may, indeed, feel lonely. But at least we do have the satisfaction of being in control. If we give up those satisfactions, we fear we might still have the loneliness, and not the other satisfactions. If we give up ourselves, we might have nothing left. If we die on our crosses, we might not rise again on the third day, or ever. That fear of dying is the root reason why we try to "keep a piece of ourselves to ourselves". Women cling to the need for verbal intimacy, using sexual control as a way to manipulate men into it. And men cling to the need for sexual intimacy, using verbal restraint as a way to manipulate women into that.

That fear of death, that fear of dying to self, is exactly what sacramental marriage asks us to confront. It is no small thing to be called to sexual intimacy. It means giving up some of our most cherished and deepest opinions. It means going against our culture in our views of what it is to be a man, what it is to be a woman. It means giving up the comforts of fitting in with other people and their values. It means, truly, dying and rising. And the first step is the one we have just seen Sarah and Dick take: the step of self-awareness, of recognizing in ourselves, and in each other, the restraints we put on our passion. We may have meant well by these restraints, we may have thought that we were doing the right thing. But the change has to begin with honest confrontation with some unpleasant truths about ourselves. We have to see in ourselves the sin of Adam, the self-primacy that the sacramental life of the Church seeks to heal. For couples, that healing comes in only one way: through passion. Human love play is the gate to divine love play. And so, sexual intimacy is the way to verbal intimacy.

Our bodies are not our own, then. They are not our own when it comes to making love, and they are not our own when it comes to intimate conversation. Dick and Sarah's poor communication has not grown out of ill will. It is not due to emotional problems, either. They are a couple who have been doing their best as best they know how. Their real problem is a deficiency in their education. Once that is cleared up, they can truly begin a new life together, a life in which they will continue to grow. Over the years, they will get better and better at giving up their control of each other, better and better in abandoning themselves to passion in every nook and cranny of their life together. Passion will be unrestrained, in their conversation and in their lovemaking as well.

Sex and conversation, then, are not opposites. In fact, they go together. To make both of them as sexual as possible, and thus as intimate as possible, both spouses have to do a lot of hard work over the entire life-span of their marriage. (One wife I know exclaimed to me the other day, "Gosh, we've been working at this for ten years, and we are still manipulating each other!") A marriage follows the same law as any other living thing — it either keeps growing or it dies. Any couple who really strive for intimacy will find that they are never finished — each new growth opens up new possibilities that they had never dreamed of before. But those new possibilities are scary because deeper intimacy means deeper vulnerability. And so the tendency to fall back into old control games is a permanent hazard. Sarah and Dick soon learned that the first step toward deeper intimacy — that first scary step — is just that, a first step. The beginning is in admitting not that one's partner has to change, but that I, myself, have to change. Let's hear Sarah's description of that realization about herself:

> Yes, I like sex. But I like it on my terms. There are certain things I like to do, and certain conditions I like to have met, and when all that is satisfied, I'm Gung-Ho! At other times, I say 'Yes', but I'm not really involved. I'm just there. My voice said 'Yes', but my body said 'No'. I was thinking about what to fix for the kids' lunches the next day, or what we'll do as soon as we're finished, or something. I was just doing what a good wife does so that I could get back to my schedule.

And then came her first realization of how she needed to change:

> What kind of person am I? I've got to look to that efficient, organized and in-control person that I am because that's the person I am when I'm in bed with Dick.

Sarah's body is still somewhat her own, not completely her husband's. Her control, shown in one way by "No-Power", extends from the bedroom throughout the whole house. She is still a single, rather than a married, person, at least to some degree. Now that she knows that fact about herself, she can begin the hard work of taking on a new identity. And the first step is in rethinking the connections between sex and conversation. Actually, all human beings, of both sexes, in every kind of human relationship, need both words and actions as ways of communicating with each other. One or the other alone is not enough. Thus, we have proverbs like "Actions speak louder than words," and "What you do shouts so loudly that I can't hear what you say." Words are often cheap and easy in human life, and can be used to cover up our inner feelings rather than revealing them. But actions all by themselves are ambiguous and can have several different meanings. Thus, we need words to interpret and clarify our actions, and we need actions to reinforce our words.

Nowhere is this double need stronger, for both words and actions, than in a sacramental marriage. The most powerful mode of communication is, without a doubt, an action — the act of making love. No other human action has such an impact on us. But that action all by itself can have many different meanings. As Sarah put it, "Sometimes he wants me, sometimes he wants us, and sometimes he wants sex." Sexual intercourse can speak tender, ecstatic joy. But it can also be the supreme act of selfishness and exploitation, of manipulation and use, of anxiety about one's worth as a person. It is one bit of body language that needs as much verbal reinforcement as we can give it. A woman who knows for sure that her husband loves her, and that his lovemaking is a sign of love and devotion, still quivers with added delight when her husband puts his love into words. She may know that she is a special person to him, but she needs to hear that every day, in countless different ways, spelled out in detail. She needs to hear it most of all just when it is most difficult for Dick to say it — while they are making love.

Most of all, for Sarah to abandon herself completely to passion, she needs the assurance, day after day, that Dick trusts her with his most vulnerable feelings. She must, of course, give up her "efficient, organized, and in-control self" in order to abandon herself to passion. But she needs an insurance policy before she can do that. She needs the security of knowing that she will not be used, ignored, shut out of Dick's inner life if she does give up that control. For just as men find women using conversation to avoid sex, women find men using sex to avoid conversation. But verbal and sexual intimacy are not opposites. They go together. A couple who find themselves caught in the game that Dick and Sarah are playing are in a vicious circle, where her sexual coolness reinforces his silence, and his silence drives her to an even tighter control over the thermostat of their passion. Both have to change. But who's going to change first?

There is one important fact about circles: they have no beginning or end. Thus, to break a circle, even a vicious circle, we can begin anywhere. We don't have to untangle the beginnings of the "No-Power" game, or figure out the stages through which it developed, or try to do things in a certain order. We can begin anywhere — wherever it is easiest to begin. St. Paul, after all, spoke to both spouses as equals. He said, "Wives, your bodies are not your own, but your husbands'. And husbands, your bodies are not your own, but your wives." Hence, Dick and Sarah can look at each other as perfect equals, as complete partners in trying to live out their total gifts of themselves to each other. The insurance policies that they need in order to become vulnerable to each other were their gifts to each other at their wedding. Their insurance was the trust in which they gave their bodies to each other. It has been renewed in every act of love since then. Both, then, can have a basic trust in each other's good intentions. Then they can follow a general pattern of healing that has worked very well for many couples.

The process begins with husbands gradually learning to be more open about putting their feelings into words. Here their wives' attitude is really crucial. For the problem we are dealing with is that women wrongly demand verbal intimacy as a condition for their own passionate lovemaking, and we want to break the pattern of that demand. However, a woman's need for verbal intimacy is quite real and healthy. All human beings need to have feelings put into words by those they love and seek intimacy with. And that verbalizing of feelings, both in speaking and in writing, has to be a constant of everyday life. What is wrong in "No-Power" situations is the demand for such conversation as a precondition to lovemaking. Odd as it may sound, Sarah must stop demanding Dick's verbal intimacy in order to make that intimacy possible. He has to be able to give it freely, without a sense of being under her control.

Moreover, Dick's learning to express his feelings in words will be very gradual, taking a long time, with two steps forward and one back. Men cannot make such a change overnight. And they certainly cannot make it completely the first time they try. Human beings do not change identities at will, like turning a faucet on and off. And for Dick even to be willing to reveal his feelings more openly is a very big and scary step for him to take. It means changing his ingrained concept of what it is to be manly and virile. He needs to gradually realize that it is not unmanly to admit weakness and dependence on a woman. It is, rather, an act of great courage and adventure. Such courage is especially crucial for a man who is going to be honest with his wife about his sexual needs. For in revealing these to her, he is making himself vulnerable in the deepest possible way. He is exposing his virility totally, and risking her rejection of that. Here's how Dick began:

> The beginning of a new intimacy for us was my being able to tell Sarah what it is like to live in an atmosphere, a home, that is *her* domain instead of *ours*. I had to tell her about my anger, and especially about my loneliness. That was very difficult, because I had never shared feelings before. I had to tell Sarah about my resentment that our whole relationship seemed to be in terms of what she got out of it. If I got access to her body long enough to ejaculate, that was supposed to be enough.

That statement gives Sarah several clues about her role in their new, intimate way of relating to each other. First, it is hard for men to share feelings when they have never done so before. She needs to develop some rather delicate listening skills. She might even have to help Dick recognize his feelings. Men often think they feel angry, for example, when what they really feel is fear. And their deepest fear is one they hardly ever recognize: the fear that their sexual appetite is bestial and selfish, and that their sexual desire is, after all is said and done, a way of using women for their own pleasure.

Sarah needs, then, to begin with a new and deeper act of faith. She needs to realize that Dick's sexual desire is not an animal appetite, but instead is an exquisite, powerful, energetic expression of his tender concern for her and devotion to her. Here we are facing a true natural difference between men and women, one that has nothing to do with cultural stereotypes. It is a simple fact of biology that the actions of a man and of a woman in sexual intercourse are quite different. For intercourse to happen at all, even in a minimal, mechanical way that any other mammal might do, the male partner has to be aggressive, energetic, forceful. In order for the male to ejaculate, a certain definite amount of sheer physical tension must be built up and then discharged. Because of that physical force, the act of intercourse might seem violent when it is just the opposite. (As noted previously, when children see couples making love, they often think they are fighting.) It is paradoxical, but true: the more passionate Dick is in making love, the more he is showing his tenderness toward Sarah, his concern for her, his devotion to her, his awe at her beauty. And so, Sarah must believe that his lovemaking is just that — an act of making love, even when it is not accompanied by words of tenderness and devotion. Such words come hard to a man, and sometimes they don't come at all. And so Sarah's faith must free Dick from the false fear that he is acting out a selfish, bestial desire. She must accept his loving for what it is, without any conditions. Only then will he be free to acquire the verbal skills that she needs from him.

If Dick can make a decision, and a promise, to begin the hard, life-long work of verbalizing his feelings more clearly and more often, the way to a new and deeper intimacy will be wide open. And if Sarah can die to herself, too, in trusting their sexual activity as the language of tenderness even when it does not include the words she would like to hear, the circle of their collaborative control game will be broken once and for all. For her trust in Dick's lovemaking will build his self-esteem, so that he will be free to be more verbal. And his increasing verbal skills will deepen her trust in their sexual activity. That new trust will further free him for intimate conversation, which in turn will deepen her trust. Her passion will then be released, and so on. The two will have another circle started, in which each conversation builds their passion for sex, and each act of intercourse frees them for more intimate conversation. Perhaps *circle* is the wrong term here, for such couples do not simply go around and around on the same plane. Rather, their intimacy is a spiral, in which both conversation and sex get deeper, the level of passion gets higher, and so they go constantly upwards rather than around in circles.

That is what happened to Dick and Sarah. They felt as if they had fallen in love all over again. The romantic feelings flow as never before, not only in the bedroom but in all their life together. Their loneliness is decreasing as their intimacy grows. The problem of men's loneliness is one we seldom hear about. Thanks to the women's liberation movement, women's problems have been getting some long-needed attention. But the assumption has been that if a man ejaculates, his sexual needs have been met. One powerful myth in our culture has been that women are tender, emotional, vulnerable, intuitive, and sensitive to other people's feelings. As a result, women are good at interpersonal relationships, and marriage, as such a relationship, is a woman's game. A man's role is to earn the living and make the decisions. Such stereotypes really suggest that women are more human than men, and that men have no need for intimacy, tenderness, close loving ties with their wives.

Intimate couples could be sacraments of healing for our culture on this important point. Previously, women probably assumed control over the domestic domain because that was all that was available to them. Men once monopolized the professions and all the positions of leadership in the world. Thanks to the women's movement, wives no longer need to control their husbands in order to have some sense of power and initiative, some sense of being persons instead of things. Sacramental wives can, along with their husbands, take advantage of this new independence for women and turn to a much more difficult, and much more important, task of liberation. We could redeem our culture from the view of sexual passion that reduces men to the level of beasts. Many men, in fact, don't even recognize their own loneliness. Their lovemaking, a silent, mechanical routine, leaves them deeply lonely, their need for true intimacy not even acknowledged. Women may lie awake in bewildered frustration after such lovemaking, as their husbands turn their backs and go to sleep. But that sleep may conceal a loneliness just as deep, a sexual frustration in the true sense of that term.

A woman, then, may fear that she is loved only for her body, especially when she does not hear the complex verbal message that she needs to hear. A sense of being used, of being treated as a thing rather than a person, may be the root of her sexual control. Such control, shown in her refusing intercourse for flimsy reasons, or granting it as a calculated favor, a reward for good behavior, is quite understandable. She may be saying, "Please don't love me just for my body." But men often make the opposite plea: "Please do love me for my body!" Passion is the way to tenderness and intimacy, to compassion and sensitivity — the way to love. Passionate sex is the way to passionate conversation. St. Paul tells us that our bodies are not our own. But our bodies are not just our sex organs. They are our tongues, too, and our hearts and brains. When a man gives himself to his wife, his words are surely part of the package. And her gift includes her uninhibited passion.

Albert Einstein, the great scientist, once made a remark that showed him to be pretty perceptive about married life, too. "Women," he said, "marry in the hope that their men will change. Men marry in the hope that their women won't change. And both end up disappointed." But he was speaking of marriages as they are, not as they can be. When we speak of sacramental marriages, we are speaking of a high ideal, indeed. We are speaking of an intimacy that is both sexual and verbal, of couples living in an aura of passion that grows as time goes on. For a couple who live such a marriage, Einstein's words do not apply. For such women, marrying in the hope that their men will change by learning to verbalize their feelings, find that hope fulfilled. And men, marrying in the hope that their women won't change, in the way that all men dread — by becoming dispassionate controllers — find their worst fear to be empty as their women live in more and more passionate abandon. Thus, instead of both being disappointed, both are thrilled and delighted. They find an intimacy that is, as Our Lord promised it would be, "beyond anything we can desire or ask for".

CHAPTER FIVE

Sex Needs Nurture

> I never shared feelings before in my life, until I was handed a notebook on the Marriage Encounter Weekend that said I should write a love letter to Betty every day. But I've tried to do it. Maybe I didn't do it right the first six months. But the fact that I wrote it is what is significant. And I'm getting better at it. But there are times when Betty will say, 'Well, I'm just not ready to make love right now. We really have to talk first.' I feel like I have to *dialogue* about everything. I know it's important for you to know how I feel. But that is not the highest priority. Maybe we really need sex before we can talk. I don't mean to be Silent Sam around the house. But sometimes it is better to sex things out than talk them out.

Fred is beginning to change, and is trying to make the really deep change, to die the death of self, which makes true intimacy possible. But he has noticed something important about the relationship between sex and conversation. Both, of course, are necessary. Since we are thinking animals, we need words to interpret our body language, and actions to reinforce our words. And for couples, the chief action that reinforces their marital conversation is intercourse. But these two techniques of communication are not really equal. Sexual intimacy comes first, is more important than conversation. And so we will give it some special attention in this chapter.

One reason for our emphasis is that dialogue has gotten a lot of attention in recent years, both in Marriage Encounter and in the mental health professions. Marriage Encounter weekends focus on improving verbal communication between spouses. Couples are taught how to speak their feelings to each other, and how to write them in daily love letters. Moreover, dialogue has become the darling of the mental health professionals in the last twenty or twenty-five years. There are countless books and articles, adult education courses, workshops and symposia, support groups, and so on, that couples can turn to in order to learn the skills of verbal communication. The techniques of verbal intimacy are pretty well covered, but those of "sexing things out" are not.

Another reason to focus on sexual skills — and a special technique which we will recommend — is that our sense of touch is especially important, more so than our sense of hearing. Words are always somewhat abstract. They don't usually carry the emotional punch that actions have. Body language speaks with feelings. Our bodily movements — facial expressions, posture, breathing rate, gestures, twitches, eye movements — these give a much better indication of how we feel about people than our words do. Many people don't pay attention to such signals. But spouses have to. For body language, especially the most expressive form of it, sexual intercourse, is their most powerful mode of communication. Couples have to learn to read each other's body language. They also have to learn how to use it to show intimacy and passion. Making love is the high point of body language. It is the action in which we use our sense of touch more intensely than at any other time. Of all our five senses, touch is the most important when we are trying to decide whether something is real or not. Sexual intimacy is probably the most powerful experience we have for making us believe that love is real. There is a built-in advantage, then, to what Fred calls "sexing things out" before trying to talk them out.

But there is a third reason why sexual intimacy is more important that conversation for building intimacy between spouses. Sexual intercourse is the Church's basic requirement for a valid marriage, not the ability to verbalize feelings. Sex is sacramental, while conversation is not (except when it is part of a sexual aura). In fact, people don't have to be able to talk at all, in order to get married sacramentally. Deaf-mutes can marry, and so can people who don't speak each other's languages. When people cannot perform sexual intercourse, however, they cannot validly marry. Sex is important. Conversation is not unimportant, but it is secondary. It becomes sacramental when it grows out of, and feeds into, sexual intimacy. And the experience of Marriage Encounter couples proves this. When women begin to give up their sexual control, their husbands automatically become more verbal. In fact, a woman can still remain quite cool in the face of her husband's revelation of his feelings in words. But we defy any husband to be silent about his feelings when he is clasped in the passionate arms of a woman who gives him her all.

What we need, though, is a technique — though not a sexual technique in the usual sense of the term. There are enough sex manuals on the market to take care of that need. We do recommend such manuals to our readers, for the language of sexual intercourse is delicate and complex, and there is always room for acquiring new skills. But mechanical skills are not enough to generate true intimacy. That only comes from passion, which is a psychological skill. The nurture of passion means that couples must keep alive what they felt when they first fell in love, and what they feel even more intensely in the ecstatic moment of intercourse. They need to keep alive their urgency to belong totally to each other. That urgency certainly includes the desire for sexual activity. But it includes much more besides. Here are Betty's words on the subject:

> Why was it, that when we were courting, we would get so engrossed in each other? We felt a really strong urge to become physically entwined in the back seat of the car. Then we went to the door, kissed good night, and you left. And I just felt delicious! I just stood there, and let those feelings run rampant in me, and I could hardly wait to go out with you the next night and have those feelings all over again. Now, I don't wait for you with that anticipation. I run away from those feelings. When I am waiting for you to come home from work I don't want to experience them. It's like, well, if you pat me on the behind when you come in, I tighten up and say, at least to myself, 'Don't do that. Don't get me excited unless it's going to lead to intercourse!' I have changed. And now I have to change back again. Our passion for each other was the gift we started out with. It was what we wanted, what we gave each other at our wedding. Now, I seem to have taken it back. That's got to change.

Betty is an insightful and honest woman. She is describing the typical decline of passion during married life that all too many couples allow to happen. They allow it because they assume that that's how things should be. Betty knows better. She wants to revive her passion, and then keep it alive and growing throughout the rest of her life with Fred. But she wonders how to stimulate passion. Passion is the force that blasts us out of our self-primacy, and allows us to belong to each other, as St. Paul says we must. Usually, the way to change attitudes is to change behavior. The new behavior we propose, for all couples who wish to nurture their passion, is "Skin-to-Skin Prime Time". It is just what its name implies. A couple will spend a half hour every day, when they are at their best, lying naked together in bed and trying to commune with each other as deeply as possible. All these elements — nakedness, prime time, daily practice, are important. And so, we will look at them, one by one.

Skin-to-Skin Prime Time (abbreviated SSPT) is a type of sexual touching that is neglected by many couples, and yet it is a powerful technique of communication. It is sexual, but not necessarily genital. It definitely arouses the unique kind of feeling, the passion, that spouses have for each other. But it is not necessarily a preparation for intercourse. There is, of course, the special kind of stimulation that gets sex organs and feelings ready for intercourse. For many couples, this is the only kind of sexual touching that there is. But SSPT is different. Its purpose is a kind of sexual union that is beyond anything that words or intercourse can express. The technique was originally devised for Marriage Encounter couples, but it is a good technique for any couple who would like to deepen their intimacy. It is powerful because it combines words and body language, passion and affection.

The first step is to find the time, and not just any time, but Prime Time. Most couples don't even give sexual intercourse their best time. They leave it for last, late at night, when both are tired and already distracted by anxieties about the next day. After the dishes are done and the children put to bed, they find time for each other, even as they wind the alarm clock for the next morning. For SSPT, a couple must give each other their best. They must set aside a good period of time, a minimum of half an hour, when both are rested and relaxed. They must not be emotionally upset, distracted by their real or imagined duties, tense, anxious, or tired. They have to be sure that they won't be interrupted — not by the telephone, not by their children or pets, not by anything else. This is their special time for each other, and each other alone. Does that sound impossible? It's not. Children can be taught to respect the closed bedroom door. If they are too small, someone can come in to watch them for half an hour (couples might even take turns doing such baby sitting for each other). And telephone calls, except for real emergencies, can be put off for thirty minutes or so. Don't we ask people to call back when we are in the shower, or balancing our checkbooks? We can do the same thing when we are absorbed in each other.

The second part of SSPT is the most important — taking off our clothes. Now that may sound right away like we're getting ready for intercourse. Most of us cannot imagine being naked together for any other reason. The aim of Prime Time, however, is not intercourse, but personal presence, a sexual contemplation of each other as the persons we are, and are to each other. If we become sexually aroused, all well and good. Intercourse is not forbidden. But neither is it the purpose. That action, in fact, can be quite dispassionate and impersonal, and not lead to any personal presence or awareness at all. For personal presence and physical presence are not the same thing at all. Two people can be quite close to each other physically—in the same house, the same bed, locked in intercourse—and still be far apart psychologically.

One of my students once asked, with an earnest frown, "If a guy is making love to a girl and thinking about someone else while he is doing it, which girl is he being intimate with?" I was delighted with the question, because it showed that this young man was beginning to see the difference between physical closeness and personal communication. He didn't understand the difference completely, of course, or he wouldn't have asked the question. He would have known that a man whose body is with one woman while his mind is with another isn't being intimate with either one. For intimacy is produced by love, by passionate affection. And he certainly doesn't have any affection for the girl he is having intercourse with. If he did, he would have his mind and heart filled with her. As it is, he is just using her for his own pleasure. But he doesn't love the girl he is thinking about either, for if he did, he wouldn't be in bed with someone else.

What is personal sexual communion, then? It is primarily (not only, but primarily) psychological presence to each other. It is a passionate preoccupation with each other, a thinking about each other and caring about each other that takes first place in minds and hearts. Two people can have that presence when they are physically far apart from each other. In fact, intimate spouses do have that personal communion all the time, even when they separate to go about their daily work, to take a long trip and so on. But their presence is most complete, most intense, and most satisfying when it is both physical and psychological. And that is what Prime Time aims at. They need not have intercourse, though they certainly may do that. But they must be as close physically as they can. And only nakedness allows for that closeness. Taking off our clothes makes every inch of us available to each other.

Couples who practice this technique testify that they find surprising riches in each other. Even those who have a special awareness of each other all the time, find that, wonderful as it is, there is something even more wonderful: there is a realization of each other so much deeper than their usual intimacy, that they are continually surprised by it. It is deeper than the presence they feel just by being home together in the evening, talking, reading the paper, watching TV together. By giving each other such single-minded attention, they find a new desire. They get a whole series of new revelations of each other as sexual persons who belong to each other. Strange as it seems, a focus on sexual activity, which makes any kind of physical closeness a prelude to intercourse, often blocks this deeper kind of communion. Prime Time requires different skills, which are primarily contemplative. In this special half hour, spouses listen to each other silently, commune without words or actions, and thus find a new realization of each other that leaves them awestruck.

The power of this technique is the power of our sense of touch. Our eyes and ears occasionally deceive us, and when they do we use our sense of touch to correct them. For example, when the pavement looks wet on a hot summer day, and we want to find out if it really is, we touch it. Touch is our "touchstone" of what is real and what is not. That is especially true in interpersonal relations, where interior attitudes cannot be seen or heard directly. We know by the way in which someone touches us whether this person cherishes us or not. Prime Time is one way for couples to make the most of this touchstone, which is often neglected. Actually, how spouses touch — or do not touch — is a very good indication of the quality of their intimacy. Do they lavish on each other the signs of affection which they found irresistible when they were first in love? As they walk around the house and pass close to each other, do they welcome such close contacts? Or do they try to avoid touching, perhaps even draw back with a muttered apology if they touch accidentally? Do they hug each other, sit close together, hold hands? These wordless touches are powerful ways of maintaining an aura of passion. They have more emotional impact than all the words in the world.

That is why nakedness is so important to SSPT. It wouldn't be the same if a couple kept their clothes on and lay down side by side, even with a lot of hugging and kissing. Many caresses become possible once clothes are out of the way. The best way for two people to be in touch with each other is to touch each other. And the best way to do that is naked. If two people sit at some distance from each other and talk intimately, they may come to certain insights into each other, a kind of personal presence. If they touch each other with their clothes on, the presence has a chance to be deeper and stronger. But for the most powerful presence of all, they need to face and hold each other in complete nakedness. Nothing else they can do, short of intercourse, can make it so vividly clear that they belong to each other. Naked holding rivets their attention right where it ought to be: on each other as man and woman.

Couples may be tempted to say that such moments are not normal. Exactly. But *normal* has two different meanings. Sometimes it means what is usual or common, what happens most of the time. In this sense, a doctor might say that it is normal for a toddler to have six colds in the winter. But in its other meaning, *normal* refers to what is right or ideal, what ought to be. This kind of normalcy is what we use as a standard for measuring what is usual or common. In this sense, a child who has even one cold is not normal, but sick. Well, then, what is normal for spouses? A daily oblivion in which passion cools, and the two forget their marital identities may be usual and common. But it is not the ideal. Prime Time, then, with the couple's awed awareness of each other, and of the depths of belonging, is more normal than the rest of a their time. If naked holding and contemplation make spouses seem not to be themselves, then Prime Time has achieved its purpose. Actually, they are more themselves then than when they are their "normal" selves. Sexual intimacy is not meant to happen only episodically, in special moments, but to be a constant. Prime Time aims at that constancy. It is a technique by which couples gradually learn to be at all times what they are at their special times, their times of falling in love and making love.

Prime Time, then, if it is to really be Prime, will have to take first priority in a couple's planning of their daily schedule. They will have to set that time first, and then arrange everything else around it. That is not as hard as it sounds. I know one couple in a Weight Watchers class who found time for their required exercise by getting up half an hour earlier in the morning to go bicycling. Intimate couples can set their alarms earlier, too. In fact, just this challenge — of finding a half hour every day for nurturing sex — will bring about greater intimacy. It will force many other decisions, and will lead couples to really clarify the priorities of their life together. As they make these decisions, their passion will be strengthened and become more of a climate than a series of episodes. And they will soon see where they are giving priority to something else besides their growth in passionate intimacy.

My husband and I had such a discussion one day that was quite amusing. He had been sick with the flu for some time, so that we hadn't been able to have our Prime Time. Meanwhile, I had gone on with my work and other interests. But one morning, he woke up and announced that he was feeling well again. I jumped at the chance — sort of. I said:

> Oh! I'm glad to hear that. Could we plan some time alone together today? Let's see. I'm going out for my daily walk right now. When I get back, our housekeeper will be here. By the time she leaves, the kids will be home from school, and I have some typing to do after they go to bed. Hmm. A busy day. Not much time for us, is there? (Sarah isn't the only efficient, organized, controlling woman in the world.) But we really haven't seen much of each other lately, and I've missed that. I know! Could we go out to lunch together?

Ed was about to agree to a lunch date when I suddenly realized what I was saying. I laughed a little, and then said,

> Wait a minute. Did you hear what I just said? I must be crazy or something. Why don't I just take my clothes off and get right into bed with you now? First things first!

Ed welcomed me with a delighted grin, and our usual half hour turned into a full hour. First things first indeed!

Without some sort of regular time for such sexual presence, there is no way in which spouses can discover each other in any depth. We have to suspend business in order to give our attention to each other, to allow our feelings to flow, to speak spontaneously instead of in a routine and programmed fashion. Prime Time, then, is not meant to be programmed intimacy. There is no such thing. There is no guarantee that even our very best efforts will succeed, for the ways of our minds and feelings are mysterious and beyond our control. And marital intimacy is a gift of the Spirit, Who breathes where He will. We can't program Him, either. And so, we ought to expect some SSPT sessions that do not bring any spectacular new insights. But the main thing is to try.

Even the quiet and unspectacular times have a deep, unifying effect, though. Each moment of such intimacy is a grace, which renews and strengthens the desire on which it lives. And sexual feelings, let us recall, are promptings of the Spirit. If we are going to respond to these with all our hearts, we must learn to recognize them. And we will learn that only if we make the effort to clear our minds of everything else, and be in each other's sexual presence as simply and as completely as we can. As we let ourselves feel these sexual impulses, we discover nuances about each other that bring an exquisite delight which cannot be discovered in any other way.

Nakedness, then, is essential to reinforcing sexual intimacy during Prime Time because it gives us full use of our sense of touch. It puts us in touch with each other in a unique way. Prolonged nongenital touching, in fact, may be more powerful, more effective in making spouses present to each other than intercourse. This is especially true of intercourse that is hasty and shallow, performed in a distracted and mechanical way when we are busy, anxious, or tired. Prime Time concentrates attention wonderfully. During this exercise, it is simply impossible for spouses to think of themselves as detached individuals, or as independent egos who belong to no one but themselves. Everything they see, hear, taste, touch and smell tells them otherwise. The SSPT experience pulls all the senses together. In their caressing and cuddling, spouses see nuances in each other's eyes that are not visible at any other times. They hear a subtle tenderness in their voices, and feel each other's warmth and strength suffusing their entire selves.

Other important things happen, too, when people take off everything except their wedding rings. Being naked together is a powerfully symbolic action. It is even more powerful if, instead of undressing themselves, the two undress each other. For when we let someone take off all of our clothes, in order to look at us, listen to us, and touch us in every possible way, we are saying, in effect, "Go ahead, I trust you. I won't hold anything back. Let's not have any barriers between us, no walls of any kind." Some spouses, in fact, don't feel totally comfortable any other way. A clothed embrace, even one in pajamas or underwear, feels like a limited, inhibited one. It seems to say, "I don't want to go all the way with you. I want to keep some distance, to hold something of myself in reserve. I want some sort of shield between us."

This symbolism of nakedness is the other side of the coin of our wearing clothes. Clothes, too, are a powerful symbol. We don't wear them just to protect ourselves from the weather; they send messages to those who see them. A classic example is the unisex style that has been popular among young people since the 'sixties. Young men and young women often dress alike, and wear their hair alike, so that the rest of us cannot tell at a glance who is which. Their style of dress is a way of rebelling against the emphasis on sex and sexual stereotypes which pervade our culture. Jeans are another example. When I was in college, girls wouldn't dream of wearing jeans. They were a reminder of the farm, which we were trying to escape from. Now, college students have to wear jeans. They telegraph a desire to belong to the group, to be accepted. Jeans are the uniform of the "in group".

Nakedness sends a message, too. It says, "I have nothing to hide." Better yet, it says, "I have nothing that I wish to hide from you." Couples with highly developed verbal skills may think that such messages are unimportant. They regularly bare their souls to each other in conversation. But they should think again. Perhaps their dialogue is not as all-revealing as they believe. Of course, others may do the opposite — they may bare their bodies in order to avoid baring their souls. They are the ones who think that intercourse is enough, and dialogue is not needed. Both kinds of couples will find something new in a daily half hour of naked cuddling. For once passionate spouses have taken each other's clothes off, they will feel an irresistible urge to come closer together, to hug and embrace as tightly as they can. It seems ridiculous to look at each other from across the room, or sit on opposite sides of the bed or even at arm's length and talk. A naked body is a magnet to another naked body. And so it should be, as one passionate person is a magnet to another passionate person.

The reason why nudity speaks so clearly of total belonging is that it exposes our primary sexual characteristics, our sex organs. And that is something we do not do in other relationships. It emphasizes that the relationship between spouses is not like their relationship with anyone else in all the world. We may have people other than our spouses that we are close to—people we love and care about, people we have fairly deep intimacies with. We belong, in various ways, to our relatives and friends, colleagues and associates. But the way that we belong to our spouse is different. It is total, and it is sexual. When we are naked before each other, we emphasize both of those facts. Usually, we conceal our sex organs in our daily contacts, even with our spouses. We have a certain sexual awareness all the time, of course. We notice who is a man and who is a woman, and relate to them accordingly. But sexual awareness, even between spouses, is usually focused on secondary sexual features: body strength, pitch of voice, facial hair, and so on. And we keep our sexual feelings under wraps. The world's work would hardly get done without these restraints.

But in Prime Time, spouses do something different. This is when we reveal our special, total belonging to each other precisely as a man and a woman. Sex organs are now in focus. In our nakedness, we say,

> I may be close to other people, but I do not face them in this particular way. My intimacy with you is not like any other. We are not together because we work well together, or have good communication, or share common interests. We are together because of sex. I desire you as a man, and you desire me as a woman. Sex is what brought us together in the beginning, and sex is the reason why we are together now.

Can you think of any better symbol? What else could say more clearly and more powerfully that two people wish to belong to each other in a total sexual intimacy? And that is exactly what the sacrament of matrimony is all about.

Physical nakedness, then, brings psychological nakedness with it. Most of us play little games with each other during the day, using poses and dishonesties to conceal our true thoughts and feelings from each other. But when clothes come off, these little deceptions won't work. A naked body says,

> O.K., here I am. I trust you to see me just as I am, as the man or woman that I am, with these sexual features and these sexual re-

sponses. And I am comfortable, even eager, in doing it because I know that you love me just for the person that I am. So, here it is. It's all yours.

Eventually, spouses will notice a big change in their relationship. They will find what is real between them when they are naked together, and that honesty will teach them how to reveal themselves to each other all the time. The little games of deception will fall by the wayside. Who needs them? Soon the intimacy that they experience during Prime Time becomes the constant atmosphere in which they live all their life together.

Gradually, even their conversations change. Every encounter becomes tender. Every conversation is a time of total attention to each other. All fears that a spouse is being coy or deceptive melt away. Their trust, their passion, their openness to each other suffuse their whole life together. When they begin SSPT, that special half hour is unlike the rest of their time together. It is a "peak experience" of intimacy. But eventually, all their time becomes prime. The psychological nakedness that they enjoy then continues even after they put their clothes on and go about their business. They belong just as deeply to each other, even as they go on to separate jobs for the day, or are separated for longer periods of time. They are as passionately present in each other's minds and hearts, sexually intimate, when they are shopping, doing house work, or whatever else they do. They come to have truly marital identities.

But what do you *say* to a naked lady? Intimacy is frightening, and sexual intimacy is especially so. As Holden Caulfield, the hero of *Catcher in the Rye,* put it, "I don't understand sex too good. You never know where you are with it." The first few times a couple face each other naked, with a half hour of uninterrupted time before them, they may just look at each other and wonder, "What now?" They may even feel embarrassed, for they are not used to this kind of communication. They may engage in intercourse simply because they don't know what else to do. They may not have verbal skills. And they may not know the skills of nongenital sexual touching and caressing either. In fact, the very possibility of a passionate man and woman being in bed together with their clothes off and not making love may seem incredible.

But what is wrong with intercourse, especially the slow, relaxed kind that is possible during Prime Time? Couples may well find that they make love more often, especially if they have let themselves be distracted from it by getting too busy with other things. And if they find themselves moving into intercourse just because they don't know what else to do, or what to say, they will have discovered something important about themselves and their marriage. They will realize, as they might not have in any other way, how restricted their sexual intimacy has been. And that realization is the first step toward growing into new way of experiencing each other.

We can't predict just what they will learn, for what they will learn is each other—a reality that is complex and mysterious, constantly changing, different for each individual and each couple. Even couples who think they know each other very well, who can finish each other's sentences, who know each other's secrets, will be surprised at what they discover about each other during Prime Time. They will be reminded of their honeymoon, when they eagerly learned more and more about each other under the heat and light of passion. They will get back to their eager wish to learn everything about each other, including their childhood experiences and their political opinions. They will get back to their original fascination and will cherish little details about each other which no one else even notices. They will once again delight just in the sounds of each other's voices, their dimples, the twinkles in their eyes. There was a time when he didn't care what she said, just so she said it. She could recite the alphabet and he would say, "Wonderful! No one ever did that so beautifully before!" There was also a time when she quoted him as an authority on any possible subject. This fascination with each other will be revived and will be kept alive by SSPT. There is an axiom among men that women are mysterious. Women, on the other hand, often brag that they know their men like the back of their hands. Prime Time makes it clear that both have infinitely mysterious depths to be explored. Falling in love is but the beginning of a voyage of discovery that never ends.

Isn't it amazing that we get over something which we thought we would never get over: that a certain special person gave himself or herself over to us in a passion which seemed like it would last forever? How could we have let that die? How is it that sexual fires die down or even die out? Yet such oblivion is exactly what most couples settle into—the daily oblivion of taking each other for granted. It is the most prevalent of all the social diseases we could name. But such oblivion has a sure prevention, and a sure cure—a daily half hour of naked cuddling and love talk, aimed at the deepest possible personal presence of each other. The attitude that we already know all that we need to know, or all that there is to know, is the world's greatest self-fulfilling prophecy. To those couples who are bored because they seem to have reached the end of their discovery of and delight in each other, we say, "Try it, you'll like it." Life together may seem a familiar landscape at times. But if we look more closely, we will see that it is instead a miniature or microcosm. It is a little masterpiece of our own creation, and if we but give it the attention it deserves we will see in it one fascinating detail after another.

Prime Time is, in fact, a daily renewal of a couple's wedding. Many couples laugh when they think back to their wedding day. How anxious they were in their planning, how careful to have the music just right, the clothes perfectly matched, the right people there, the ritual properly performed! And yet, when the day actually came, what was in the forefront of their minds? Nothing but each other. (I have never been able to remember whether or not the organist played the music I asked for at my wedding. In fact, I can't remember what it was that I asked for.) In the face, and in the touch, of each other everything else faded into the background. What they were to each other in that moment is what they remember the most as the years go by. Prime Time is a most fitting *memento* of their wedding. In the Bible this word has a stronger meaning than what we usually give it. We mean a memory, a recollection of something over and done with. But in the Bible, a memento, like the Eucharist as a memento of the Last Supper, is a way of making something real and present all over again, of reenacting a past event in the here and now. Thus Prime Time is a memento of that special moment in which each one's attention was fully given to the other, when passion drew them to desire nothing else than their total belonging to each other.

Such a memento is necessary every day. Spouses are usually separated, at least for the length of a working day. During these separations, their explicit, top-level attention is on other things. They have to think about their tasks and products, the people they associate with, their children, the practicalities of getting from here to there, and so on. Thus, when they come together again, they need what is called a "reentry ritual", some way of making the transition from being apart to being together again. We human beings cannot shift our attention, and especially not our feelings, from one focus to another as quickly as we can turn a faucet on and off. We need not only some time to readjust, but some sort of ritual or symbolic action (like the old pipe and slippers routine) to ease ourselves out of one environment and into another. Dr. George Bach, the famous psychologist, once described his reentry ritual on the Phil Donahue show: when he comes home from work, he sits in his favorite chair, has a martini, and "doesn't have to listen to anybody for an hour". He is not staying distant from his wife and family. It is his way of tuning out his work world and moving slowly, with full attention and feeling, into the world of his family.

Many married couples are careless about their partings and their returns. They say "Good bye" for the day, and "Hello" for the evening in a perfunctory way. But such inattention is really a carelessness about their intimacy. They should be more careful of, more caring about, their separations and reunions. It is natural to give each other a debriefing on the day's events when they come together again at the end of a day. But without some sort of reentry ritual, their intimacy may remain out of focus. Friends and roommates, after all, debrief each other, as do brothers and sisters. But to a couple, sex is what is important. If sex has faded into the background, then sex is what has to be brought back to the foreground. The main thing is to reestablish their marital identities. The debriefing is not bad, of course. It is important. It is, in fact, essential to intimacy for people to know what each has been doing while they were separated. There are some marriages in which this is not the case. Some wives have no clear idea of what their husbands do all day at their jobs (and vice versa). Such couples are not really living a common life. Their intimacy, if they have any at all, is quite poor. Their passionate presence to each other is far from constant. All couples, then, have to "catch up on the news" that each has to report if they are to live in passionate intimacy.

But their debriefing, their sharing of the day's news, ought to have a true marital quality to it. And that means it has to be passionate. It cannot be the calm kind of discussion that either one might have with just anybody. So, the first item on the agenda ought to be the renewal of their passion. And that is where SSPT comes into the picture. It is the best possible reentry ritual, better than pipe and slippers, better than a silent hour with a drink in a restful chair. Maybe it is not possible to schedule a half hour of Prime Time at the moment of their reunion at the end of a day. Prime Time may have to be after supper, in the middle of the night, or early in the morning. But there are two important cautions. The first is that a couple not let themselves slip into a pattern where all of their conversation is about the news of the day, and none is about themselves and their relationship with each other, their passion for each other. We believe such a nonmarital pattern is rather common among couples. When they end their debriefing for one day, they begin planning activities for the next, and never get around to the real issue — which is their passion.

The other caution is for couples who do practice SSPT. These spouses will have to resist the temptation to chatter about the day's events during their special time of naked cuddling. They will, of course, have many things to talk about. They may also have angry issues to resolve or decisions to make. But all of this must be put aside so that they can concentrate on their passion. Anything else is a distraction. During much of Prime Time they may not want to talk at all. But if they do, their talk must be about only one subject: themselves and their passion. They must talk about their desire for each other at that moment, their memories of past desire, their hopes for future desire. They can recall their particularly close moments of the past—it is surprising how the meaning and joy of these can deepen as time goes on. Never mind that they have talked of them dozens of times before. Never mind that each knows, and knows that the other knows, how they felt about each other then, and how they feel about each other now, and how they hope to feel about each other years from now. The very act of putting these feelings into words is a powerful way of making them stronger. And they always take on new meaning in the context of a new day.

"I am so glad I married you—more so than ever before." Those words will never have a routine, repetitious meaning, even if they are spoken every day. "Guess what happened to me today?" is not a good conversation opener for Prime Time. This is especially true if these words are spoken in anger, bringing up some painful issue between the two spouses. There are lots of legitimate grievances, disagreements, and hurts that intimate couples have to negotiate. It is deadly to any kind of human intimacy to have these suppressed. But we are suggesting a different approach. Usually an aggrieved spouse will say, "No you don't. Don't you touch me, don't you come close to me, until we get this settled. We are not friends right now." In other words, conversation first, and then sex. That order of things is backwards, especially when it happens during Prime Time. In fact, an intimate couple are always friends, always close, always ready to touch and be touched, even when one has some legitimate grievance or disagreement with the other. That's what the aura of sexual intimacy means. Intimate couples don't say, "We're not friends right now." They are always friends. They don't say, "We have to settle this before we can be close." They are always close.

What, then, do they say? We certainly don't suggest that Prime Time be a way of avoiding issues and grievances. Nor do we mean that these are suspended while spouses enjoy some sex play, and then resume their angry confrontation afterwards. In fact, we can use this example of anger to understand the depth of conversion that SSPT aims at. It is the same deep conversion that the sacrament of matrimony aims at. It is the same deep conversion that all Christians have to experience in order to be saved. The idea that two people have to resolve their grievances in verbal confrontation before they can love each other is as wrong for other Christians as it is for spouses in their naked half hour together. The order needs to be reversed. Instead of negotiating first and then loving after, we love first, and thus let love be the context of our negotiations. For spouses, this loving context is sexual. A couple who would first talk out their anger, as a condition for feeling passionate, would create a caricature of Prime Time and of sexual intimacy.

When one spouse is angry, the other is often apathetic. For example, when a wife greets her husband with a demand to know why he didn't call her from work, he may well be impotent in their next lovemaking. Anger and apathy are ways of avoiding intimacy, of holding ourselves to ourselves instead of belonging to our spouse. But Prime Time is an excellent way to heal both of these wounds in a couple's intimacy. As Fred said, sometimes it is better to sex things out than to talk them out. What a couple must do, then, when one is angry and the other withdrawn, is to seek each other out for a session of naked cuddling and affectionate, passionate conversation about their love for each other. This session will renew their sexual presence, their gifts of themselves to each other. When their passion is renewed, they will be ready to discuss whatever they need to discuss. Their conversation will then be intimate rather than hostile, because their passion will keep them in their marital communion. Only when their bodies are not their own, but each other's, can they settle grievances and differences. For in the glow of passion, the angry spouse will no longer be looking for a hurtful revenge. The words, "Why didn't you call me today?" have two quite different meanings, and can be spoken in two quite different tones. When spoken in the angry tone of a woman whose passion has cooled, they sound like an accusation, a desire to return a hurt for a hurt. But those very same words, spoken in the aura of passion, by a wife who knows she is cherished and is awed by a tender realization of that fact, mean something entirely different. "Why didn't you call me today?" is then a simple request for information that will enable her to carry her beloved more constantly in her heart. She wants to know so that she can have a more vivid mental picture of what he does when he is physically away from her. And that is information which he, in his passion, will be eager to give her.

Many couples sense a rhythm of ups and downs in their life together. Even those who don't fight and then reconcile find peaks and valleys of another kind. There are times when their intimacy is luminously real and suffuses all the rest of life. In those times, passion is at its peak, friendships are happy, music is sweet, jokes are funny, children are charming, and prayer seems to be their constant state. In their low periods, all of this is reversed. Passion seems dormant, perhaps even dead. Friends seem distant, music loses its charm, jokes lose their humor, children are irritating, and prayer is out of the question. When we have this roller coaster experience, we wish we could live on the peaks all the time, and never descend to the valleys. But often, when we sense this rhythm, we also sense that we don't have any control over it. We can be on a peak one day, and in a valley the next, without knowing why or how we got there. Skin-to-Skin Prime Time is a technique which can give us precisely the control that we want. It gives us a way to make the peaks more frequent and long lasting, so that the heights and depths of sexual intimacy can be our whole state of being. For the roller coaster rhythm that we sense is the rhythm of sin and grace. The valleys of dispassionate plodding, when intimacy seems to have no real substance to it, are the times when we withdraw into our sinful self-primacy. In those times, our bodies are our own, and we belong to no one but ourselves. The peaks are times of redemption, when passion draws us out of ourselves into an intimacy that is so real that we cannot doubt it for a moment. It is no mystery, then, that Prime Time can create an aura of sexual intimacy for all the days of our lives. For Prime Time is the way to passion. It is the uncovering of sexual desire, and of total belonging, with nothing held back, and nothing between us. That belonging is the grace of the sacrament of matrimony. And like any other grace, it heals the sin of clinging to ourselves. Couples who have wondered, in their peak moments, "Why can't we be like this all the time?" don't need to wonder any more. With Skin-to-Skin Prime Time, they will know that they can be like that all the time. And they will know in a very practical and concrete way, how to do it.

CHAPTER SIX

Sex Nurtures Children

Mom, what would you say if I told you I'd like to look at a copy of Playboy *magazine?*

Fourteen year old Bill was home from school with a bad cold, and alone with his mother for the first time in many months. What would she say to such an honest, direct question on such an important topic? Her reaction could have a deep and long lasting effect on her son's sexual development. Would she shout an angry "No — and don't you ever ask such a question again!"? Would she perhaps hem and haw, her own embarrassment embarassing her son, too? Either of these responses might cut off communication between them. On the other hand, if she just said, casually, "Sure, I'll go get one for you," he might think that sex is just another form of entertainment. He might not realize that it is such a powerful force for human intimacy and salvation.

Bill's question posed a dilemma that many parents of the current generation of teenagers find themselves in. As one mother put it, at a parent's meeting at my son's high school, "We don't say much about sex to our son. We're afraid of handing on the hang-ups we were raised with. And yet, we don't know what to put in their place." In fact, the whole area of moral teaching in Catholic circles seems to be in disarray these days. And this is especially true in regard to sexual morality. We all know that our children need much more guidance than they are getting, both at home and at school. But we don't quite know how to give them what they need. We know it's important to have open communication with our children. But what to communicate is a harder question. And we also know of powerful forces in our children's culture that seem to overwhelm anything we try to do at home.

The best hope in this situation is for parents to cultivate and nurture their own sexual passion for each other. For passion changes everything.

It changes their own way of looking at sex. It builds their own self-confidence and self-esteem. It gives them an insight into their own childhood and adolescence, especially their sexual development (or lack of it.) But most importantly, it strengthens the bond of affection for their children in a wonderful way. And that is the main help that children need for their own development, sexual and otherwise, especially in their teenage years. Growing up, after all, is an identity change. And passionate parents, having experienced such a change themselves, have some understanding of it. They have some sympathy for others who, like their children, have several such big changes ahead of them. We won't guarantee that the sex education of their teenagers will be easy, that they will always know the right things to say. Nor can we quite guarantee that the parents will be able to hand on their religious beliefs to their children, along with their sexual attitudes. But we can guarantee that their sexual intimacy will create an atmosphere in their home in which these beliefs and attitudes will be fostered. And we can absolutely guarantee that growing up in an atmosphere of sexual intimacy is, next to life itself, the most precious gift that parents can give to their children. It will do more than anything else to give them a basic contentment with life, and a solid belief in the reality of human love. Passion preaches the gospel in the home, and preaches it effectively.

Many couples think that, once their first child is born, they have to find ways to integrate their new parental role with their marital role. They know that their relationship to each other is now different, and wonder about the relationship between their love for each other, with its strong sexual component, and their love for their children, which is primarily a nurturing devotion. Unfortunately, the solution which many couples give to this problem is to put their own passion on the back burner for a few years. They mean well. Their plan is that later on, when the nest is empty, they will pick up again where they left off with each other. But during the years of having and raising their children, they will be parents first and lovers second, when they can fit it in. As they live out this plan, giving parenthood priority over sexual intimacy, they find their time and attention taken more and more by their loving concern for their children, and they may go for weeks, months, even years without having any time alone together.

The tragedy in this choice is, of course, that passion soon cools, perhaps even dies, and with it their lover and beloved identities that passion had forged. The two become single parents. But later on when they try to resume their interrupted intimacy, they find that it is not as easy as they thought. They have little to talk about, and even seem to be strangers, needing to get acquainted with each other all over again. But there is a still deeper tragedy here: in their misguided effort to be good parents, to nurture their children in every way, they have deprived their children of what they need the most. For, more than anything else, children need the nurture of their parents' passion for each other. Without that, they are living in a single-parent family. True, they have two single parents instead of just one. But they miss out on what they most need in their childhood, just as surely as if their parents were legally and physically separated.

The sexual intimacy of parents is the power base of their children's identities, including their sexual identities. It grounds their emotional health and maturity, their overall enjoyment of life, and their faith in the God Who is Love. Children who, no matter how good their parents' intentions, are deprived of a passionate home suffer in every way—emotionally as well as religiously. Their identities are confused and insecure, and they easily feel a general distaste for life. They assume a disbelief in the reality of love, and thus in the reality of the God Who is Love. In order to see this multiple tragedy more concretely, let's look at the process of decision making in a passionate home, for we know that bringing up children means making one decision after another.

The president of a Jesuit High School said it very well. He was giving the homily at a mass for the mothers of his students. He knew what he was talking about, and we nodded and even wept a bit as he told us what it is like to be the mother of an adolescent boy. He knew how our sons drop verbal bombs on us and then seem to have forgotten them the next day. He knew, as we did, that at other times a quiet phrase which we scarcely hear might indicate one of our son's most serious problems. But we Catholic mothers, he pointed out, have an advantage that other mothers don't have: the grace of the sacrament of matrimony. "That grace does not guarantee that you will always make infallibly right decisions. But it does guarantee you something else, something more important: the ability to love always." He was right. And that grace is passion.

When parents make decisions about their children, these decisions should come out of the parents' passion for each other. If they do, they will be right decisions, even when they are incorrect. But if they do not, they will be wrong decisions, even when they are correct. Decisions about budgeting time and money, about choosing schools, about guiding friendships and dating, about sex education, and family prayer, are all marital decisions. They are parental, of course, but in order to be parental, they must first be the decisions of two people who live passionately in each other's minds and hearts. The first step, then, for any couple making any decision about their children should be a quick checkup on their passion for each other. Have they allowed themselves to drift into a state of cooled-off passion? Is there, perhaps, some unresolved grievance keeping them apart? If their intimacy seems intact, they are ready to make the decision. If it is not, they must first repair it, first restore their passion. Prime Time will often be their first step toward decision making.

Passionate parents, then, do not approach their children's care directly. They do not ask, "What is the best thing for this child?" They ask instead, "What is the best thing to do for promoting our own intimacy?" What is best for any child is always his parents' passion for each other. Suppose a couple are choosing a high school for one of their children. Such a decision raises many questions. They have to ask about the location of the school. They have to ask about its religious or secular character, and its level of academic excellence. They need to know whether it is coeducational or just for students of one sex. They need to consider its various programs, and how these match up with the talents and interests of their child. And of course financial considerations are important, too.

But there are two different ways in which a couple might go about answering all of these questions. A dispassionate couple who, with good intentions, have put their passion on the back burner, will approach the questions one by one, weigh the pros and cons, and come up with a decision. They then put their time and energy into carrying out the decision. They have the illusion that they have made the right decision. But they have make a very basic mistake: they have deprived their child of the sexual aura which gives him his identity. It is their own passion that gives his talents and interests their basic value. The couple may decide, for example, that Johnny needs to go to a school that has a special music program that suits his individual needs. But it is so expensive and far away that the mother will have to take on a job to help their finances. With her working, she and her husband will have precious little time for cultivating their romance. But they make that sacrifice, "for Johnny's sake". Poor Johnny! He would be better off in a school closer to home, one whose costs would not detract from his parent's passion, even if the school did not have the special music program.

Another couple, let us say, put their sexual intimacy first. After a session of Skin-to-Skin Prime Time, they begin to discuss which high school would be best for their child. After looking at all the factors involved, all the same factors that the other couple looked at (for these are, after all, the important questions, once passion is ensured), they decide on the school that seems the best. For example, my husband and I were offered a scholarship to a New England prep school for our adopted biracial son. It would have set him on the road to Harvard Law School, perhaps, or medicine, with all the opportunities that such a background might bring. But we chose to keep him at home, in the aura of our passion, instead. He will have a much better chance of becoming a man who believes in love and lives in it, who believes and lives in the God who is Love, than if he would spend his teenage years in a boarding school. And being that kind of loving person is more important than any career we can name.

Passionate parents do make mistakes, as many as any other parents. Sex does not guarantee infallibility. But even when passionate parents do make mistakes, their decisions are basically right. They grow out of, and feed back into their sexual intimacy. And that intimacy is the most important element of the nurture that their children need. No matter how much a child's talents and interests might be developed, he will be a deprived child if he does not grow up in a passionate home. The mistake of choosing the wrong school is minor in comparison to the tragedy of depriving children of a passionate home. When sexual love is present in his home, all's well with a child. When it is not, nothing is.

Now let's look briefly at the usual path of normal human development, especially in childhood and adolescence. A child is born knowing nothing about himself and nothing about the world. He does not know who he is, or who other people are. He doesn't know what life is all about, whether it is basically good or bad, whether the world is friendly or hostile. He gradually forms answers to all of these questions as he experiences more and more of life. The early years of childhood are very important years, because in them we have our first experiences, formulate our first answers to all these questions. And these answers stay with us into adult life. A young child is not, of course, aware in any clear and self-conscious way that he is forming views about the meaning of human life. But that is what he is doing. Psychologists have learned that unhappy experiences in childhood can cause a child to grow up fearful, suspicious, hostile, insecure, angry—unable to give and receive love. Sometimes with great effort these negative attitudes can be healed later in life. But often they are not. There are many, many unhappy, unloving adults in the world who come to be that way because their parents allowed their passion to cool.

A banner that we often see in our churches proclaims, "THE BEST THING A FATHER CAN DO FOR HIS CHILDREN IS TO LOVE THEIR MOTHER." That motto is perfectly true, for the grace of the sacrament of matrimony works through the laws of human psychology.

When a couple cherish their own sexual intimacy as the main focus of their life together, then they are not depriving their children of love, or even of time and attention. In fact, they are doing the best possible thing for their children's psychological growth.

The main task in anyone's growth as a person is to establish his identity—to know clearly who he is as a person, so as not to confuse himself with someone else, or try to be like someone else. He must find his own true individuality. Children often complain, and rightly so, when their parents try to force them into an identity that is not theirs. As a college professor, I have known quite a few unhappy students who were aiming toward medical school or law school, not because they wanted to or because they had any talent for those professions, but because they were under pressure from their parents to follow in their fathers' footsteps. I have known many other students who were in college simply because their parents insisted that they go to college, and not because they had any desire for learning. And of course we all know of the tragic case of David Kennedy, who claimed in an interview shortly before his death that he became involved in drugs because he could not handle the pressure of "being a Kennedy". He was expected to do certain things for which he had no inclination. All of these are examples of children trying to find their true identities.

This task is hard enough for all of us, without the additional pressures from parents trying to set identities for us. Parental pressure on children usually comes from parental insecurity. Dispassionate parents who have not found their own secure identities often use their children to satisfy their own emotional needs. The remedy for pressured children, then, is sex—the renewal of their parents' passion. When, as passionate lover and beloved, couples make each other the focus of their life together, they automatically establish their own true identities. They are not primarily care givers or disciplinarians. They are not primarily parents. That role grows out of their total belonging to each other. When they delight in their mutual identity, they automatically take a lot of pressure off their children.

Their passion immediately, and forever, establishes the identities of their children. That passion is what brought their children into existence as the unique individuals which they are, and that passion is what will sustain them in their special identities all through their lives. Even if their parents should die, the memory of their passion will enable their children to remain secure in being who they are—the sons and daughters of two special people who came together because of a very special feeling for each other.

Scholars often argue about which is more important in making a child turn out to be the kind of person he is as an adult: heredity or environment. The question is really unanswerable, though, because no two people have exactly the same heredity except, perhaps, identical twins. The genetic makeup of children of the same parents varies quite a bit. Those who are raised in the same family do not have the same environment, either. Two siblings, say a boy and a girl, have different positions in the family, and are treated differently as a result. The girl will have a brother but not a sister, and the boy will have a sister but no brother. One of them will be older than the other, and even when they share the same events, such as family camping trips or visits to relatives, each will perceive and react to those events differently, because of their different temperaments, memories, and feelings.

The heredity-versus-environment debate has no final answer. But one thing is sure: the most important factor in deciding what kind of person each child is, and what kind of adult he grows up to be, is his security in his basic identity as the offspring of his parents' sexual desire. The all-important question for all children is whether or not Mom and Dad love each other. If they do, their child will feel secure and comfortable as the offspring of that love. His stability in his own identity will be so deep that the child may never even notice it. It grows out of his parents' enthusiastic acceptance of him, their love for him, their delight in him. And they accept him as the special individual that he is, simply because he exists. His existence is, after all, the overflow of their cherished and nurtured passion for each other. And because they identify him as the fruit of their passion, they make no demands on him.

He does not have to behave in a certain way in order to win their love and approval, since he already has their love and approval, and has had it from the moment of his conception. More than that, he will have it for all eternity, for the identity he has as their child will never change. Such a child does not have to have curly hair or blue eyes in order to be loved. More importantly, he does not have to have the talents someone else has, or the tastes and interests that his parents specify, in order to be loved and cherished. He does not need to follow his father's profession in order to win approval. He is free to find out who he is and how he fits into the world, and to enjoy this. The lovableness of his true self is already assured.

To say that a child is loved and accepted just for being who he is may not seem very important, but it is. We can see how important it is if we look at children who don't receive such love. Parents often give off signals, even when they are not thinking about it, that indicate quite clearly what their basic attitude toward their children is. Watch, for example, how people handle their young children in public — literally "handle" them. Notice how they touch them, how they hold them, how they lift and carry them. Some people put their toddlers on a bus, or into a car, with a manner that is just a little rough and careless, as if they were annoyed at having to do so. They seem to have their minds on something else, as if their children were a distraction from something more important. We don't mean people who are physically cruel and abusive to their children, but those who just do not show a special tenderness and gentleness in the way that they handle them. Many people will lift a toddler by one arm, for example, to put him on a bus. Such lifting doesn't seem to injure the child or cause him any pain. But it indicates an attitude of carelessness and disrespect. Other parents carry and lift their toddlers with a gentle, almost reverent manner that shows a special care for their delicate feelings and for their precious mystery as persons.

I saw one such mother in my gynecologist's office one day. She had a brand new baby with her, surely less than a month old. But she kept up a continuous conversation with her baby, looking with awed delight into her eyes all the while. "I'm going to take your bonnet off now. There, doesn't that feel better?" "Oh, would you like me to hold you? Come on up," said the mother, gently lifting the little girl out of her infant seat. But the baby kept fussing, no matter which way the mother held her. "Gee, you just can't find a comfortable position, can you? I sure know that feeling!" That baby was obviously loved just for being, and for being who she was — the offspring of her parents' passion.

Other children are rejected, or at least not wholeheartedly accepted by their parents, simply because of the fact that they exist. They seem to be burdens to their parents. The parents treat them with a dutiful air, as if they were a constant annoyance and responsibility. As these children grow older, they get a deeper feeling of insecurity inside. It seems that their parents become annoyed with them no matter what they do. Their physical appearance is never quite right. Their parents criticize their posture, their hair styles, the way they dress. Their most innocent behavior brings a scolding. The patterns of the scoldings are bewildering, as they are scolded for doing one thing one day and for doing the opposite the next.

These children get the impression that the basic problem is their very existence. They are burdensome just because they were born and are present in the family. Such feelings are deeply discouraging and often cause serious depression in children. Even if they are not that serious, such feelings cause children to try to win their parents' affection and approval by their behavior. They choose their life's work, or adopt tastes in music and food that will please their parents, and so on. They try to take on false identities. But when these efforts to win acceptance and approval don't succeed (and children know that they don't), they become resentful. Then they use that bitter phrase, "I didn't ask to be born, you know." These words are terrible because they are perfectly true. No one of us ever asked to be born. In order to do that, we would have to know what life is and decide whether we wanted it or not, before we existed, which is impossible. Every one of us exists because someone else brought us into existence without consulting us, and give us a certain genetic makeup that is permanent and unique.

That genetic makeup is a very important part of our identities, for it does not just determine our physical appearance, such as eye color and hair texture. Our genetic makeup also has a great deal to do with our temperament and emotions, our intelligence, our talents and interests. That's why it is so devastating to a child to be criticized for things he cannot help. Dispassionate parents often use a terrible phrase when one of their children does something wrong: "What's the matter with you?" Parents who say that expect certain behavior as a condition for giving their love and approval. But what must it sound like to a child who is struggling under an impossible burden to begin with—the burden of making himself lovable—to hear, when his efforts fail, that there is something the matter with him? This common phrase may look and sound rather harmless, but it is not. It indicates a basic parental attitude: that the child's identity as a person is somehow defective.

There is another phrase that is as common and as significant: "Look at that—he's just like his father!" Or, "My goodness, you're just like your mother." Sometimes these words are an angry reprimand which are deeply disheartening to a child. Of course he is just like his father or mother! That is how heredity works. Children come to be who they are by a combination of genetic material from their parents. But what is a child to do when he is condemned for being like one of his parents? This is something he has no control over, something that was given to him without his consent. In fact, it ought to be celebrated as one of the most beautiful mysteries of the world, this mystery of heredity and parenthood.

Negative phrases are most often spoken by parents whose passion for each other has declined or died (or never existed to begin with). But parents who cultivate their romance have an entirely different view of their children. They enjoy their children, and correct and discipline them in an entirely different way. They, too, use the phrase, "You're just like your mother (or father)." But the tone of voice is different, and so is the meaning of these words. To a passionate spouse, it is a great delight to discover reflections of this beloved spouse in their children, even when these reflections are somewhat negative. A wife who is enthusiastically in love with her husband is well aware of his faults, and looks beyond them to the goodness of his person, and loves him for that. She takes the same attitude toward their children.

Does she see his sloppiness in one of their children, or her own inability to get going in the morning? Well, so what? She loves her husband so ecstatically that his sloppiness is not an issue between them. And then their sloppy child is a reminder of their passion. She is not angry, but a little amused, even delighted, when she says, "You're sloppy just like your father." Secure in the knowledge that she loves him, and he loves her, in spite of deficiencies, she will not be dismayed to see these in their child. She will love the child anyway, and even see a certain beauty in the fact that the child resembles one of his parents. That resemblance, even when it is negative, is a delightful reminder of their continuing love for each other. It renews the passion that is strong enough to see a certain beauty even in a beloved's faults.

In the words of the old song, then, passionate spouses sing, first to each other and then to each of their children, "Most of all, I love you 'cause you're you." Children of such parents find their identity tasks easy. They move through childhood and adolescence with relative ease and comfort, gradually finding out who they are and how they fit into the world, and what their vocation in life is. They enjoy, in a deep and stable way, the lovable identity that has been handed to them on a platter, as indeed it should have been. They are loved simply for being, and for being who they are — the beloved offspring of their passionately loving parents.

Brad, who was named after his father, asked his mother one day, "How come you named me Brad?"

"Well, I picked your name, really, and I named you after your Dad because I hoped that you will grow up to be the kind of man that he is."

"But I don't want to be a professor. I want to drive a truck."

"Of course. That isn't what I meant. If you want to be a truck driver, that's fine. What I meant was that I wanted you to be the kind of person that Daddy is — a man of deep religious faith, and to love people the way he does."

Children need discipline and correction, just as much as they need food and clothing and shelter. But there are two ways to go about it. Dispassionate parents constantly supervise, criticize, and correct every move their children make. When they discipline, they do so harshly, and with words that make the children feel unloved because they are unworthy of being loved just because of who they are. They perceive themselves as objects of a dutiful sense of responsibility. Passionate spouses, on the other hand, enjoy their children for being who they are. Their children are not just accidents, results of passionate moments which are long since past. Passion is not past history, but the ongoing atmosphere that they constantly breathe, a natural environment which supports their children's existence as surely as do food, air and water. These children experience the world as a great place to be in. Their home radiates joy, rather than a dutiful 'busyness' which children can hardly wait to escape from when they grow up.

One young Jesuit priest recently told a story from his life, when his father bought a long-desired new car for the family. Jeff was noted for being a very cautious driver but as he was carefully backing the car out of the garage to pick up his friends for basketball practice, he scraped the chrome off the right side of the car. His father came out to inspect the damage, and Jeff handed over the keys, bracing himself for a scolding. Instead, his father picked up the chrome, put it into the trunk, and said, "We'll take it in to be fixed tomorrow." He then handed the keys back to his son, and said, "Have a good time at your practice."

Jeff now says that, at that moment, he saw the point of the story of the Prodigal Son. The gospel had been preached in his family, and preached most effectively in the language of the passion his parents felt for each other. His father couldn't be harsh with him. He was too much in love with his mother. A less passionate husband would have been angry, and asked, "What's the matter with you?" But passion gives parents an exquisite gentleness with each other and with their children. It is bridled sex, passion that is inhibited by false fears and a dutiful approach to life, that makes parents irritable and sometimes even cruel with their children. Passionate parents are often tired. They get physically exhausted by the demands that children make on their energy. But they are never drained of gentleness and warmth, of patience and joy, at least not for long. For these are constantly fueled by their passion for each other.

Raising children, then, is a highly sexual activity, not a dispassionate, dutiful ministry. Many parents try to separate their marital and parental roles, and even think of their sexual desire as a distraction to their parenting, and *vice versa.* The wife then thinks of herself primarily as a homemaker, and the father as a provider—or they may share, or even reverse, these two roles. But the results of separating parental and marital roles is very destructive. It denies the very identities of all the people involved. We know how cruel it is in a divorce hearing for a child to be asked to choose between his parents, to live with one and reject the other. In dispassionate homes, such choices can be almost routine, as the child is asked time and again to take sides even though the parents live in the same house.

But the sexual presence of spouses in each other's minds and hearts ought to be so evident that when a child is talking to his father, his mother is also present, at least in both of their minds, as a cherished, beloved third party. Choosing between them, or playing them off against each other, isn't even considered. The child should not be able to even think of his father apart from his mother, nor his mother apart from his father. For when children are aware of their parents' passion for each other, and of the source of their own existence in that passion, they feel secure about their own identities. They know that their own lovability is as assured today as it was when they were conceived.

Such comforting clarity about their own identities doesn't always come to children through words, though these are important. Parents may not explicitly say, "Remember, your mother is my wife," or "Don't forget, the reason you exist is that your father loves me." Children do need such verbal assurances at times, to make sure that they understand the connection between their parents' love for them and their passion for each other. But the deepest reassurance comes through in less explicit ways—subtle gestures, tone of voice, ways of touching. For example, when a child sees his father give his mother an affectionate pat on the behind, and she pushes him away with a look of disgust, the child draws an immediate conclusion. The conclusion is not what we might think—"Mommy doesn't like sex,"—but, rather, "I am not lovable." And the reverse is also true: a child who sees his parents give and exchange eager little signs of passionate affection gets the message "I am loved, because Mommy and Daddy love each other."

When parents talk directly to their children, the messages are also clear. Their mother may not mention their father, or quote him; she may even be disagreeing with him on some point. But her tone of voice, and her affection for her children, will make it clear to them that their father is present just as truly in their mother's heart as if he were physically in the same room. And her presence in his desire will be just as evident when they hear him speak of her. In such homes, no one is a detached individual, allied with first one and then another detached individual, each struggling to win acceptance and approval from the others. Since the spouses belong to each other in a passion that is constant, and since that passion is the ongoing source of the identities of the children, everyone's identity is secure and clear.

Passion is thus as important to spouses after they become parents as it was before—indeed, it is more important. For all of us begin our lives as children, and need the support of our parents' passion for each other throughout our lives, even after we leave our original home and establish families of our own. The finding of our identities, and the joyful perception of these, is a task we do not complete until we come to the very end of our lives. And our parents' passion for each other is just as important to us in adulthood and old age as it was in our childhood and adolescence. A divorce is devastating to children, even when those children are full grown and parents themselves. The psychological divorce that results from muted passion is just as devastating. When passionate parents die, the memory of their sexual intimacy is a powerful support, and a necessary one, that keeps identities secure even in the years of grief. Children whose parents did not show a deep and continuing intimacy between themselves find grieving more painful, and harder to heal, because their parents' dying calls their own continuing identities into question. The moment of passion which brought them into being has come to be dead history, and their own existence something of an accident that needs to be justified in order to continue.

One important part of children's finding and enjoying their identities, without pressures to prove their worthiness to be loved, is the finding and enjoying of their sexual identities. Each child needs to understand as clearly as possible what it is to be masculine and feminine, how it is good to be either one, and which one he or she is. Girls need to feel good about being girls instead of boys, and yet know that it is good for boys to be who they are. And boys need to see the value of their own existence as boys, as well as the goodness of girls' being girls. Sex education is, of course, an important part of this process, a process that is especially crucial in adolescence, when children first feel the power of sexual feelings. But sex education begins much sooner than that.

In fact, when we allow children to talk about what they want to talk about, one finds they are interested in the most serious questions of human life almost from the time they are able to talk. If we do not put restraints on their curiosity, and do not put them down for asking questions, three-year-olds will ask about love and death, about God, and yes, about sex. And it is a basic law of educational psychology that human beings learn best when their natural curiosity makes them ready to listen. The deepest kind of sex education, then, the kind that communicates values and meaning, not just information, begins almost the moment a baby is born. Like the deepest kind of religious education, this kind of sex education is caught, not taught. It is communicated by the way that parents look at each other, speak to each other, touch each other — and the ways in which they look at, speak to, and touch their children. Passionate parents communicate passion, love, and intimacy in ways that cannot be captured in textbooks and dictionaries.

Eventually, though, children need explicit verbal information — straight talk about the so-called 'facts of life.' They need detailed information about sexual anatomy and physiology, about sexual intercourse and intimacy. Unfortunately, such sex education is still unusual in Catholic homes and in Catholic schools. One of my students once told me of a conversation in which he, his parents and his grandparents talked for two hours about sexuality and what it meant to them in their different stages of life. I am sure that such conversations are rare. They should be the order of the day in every family.

Parents hesitate to speak to their children about sex, just as much as their children hesitate to speak to them. As a result, most teenagers get their sexual values from their popular culture. But the picture of sex that our culture presents is an especially tawdry one. Sex is vulgarized in rock music, commercialized on television, trivialized in the movies. As a result, the adolescents of our day have very few sources from which they might learn that sex is awesomely beautiful, powerfully joyous, deeply redemptive, sacramentally holy. In fact, if we were to tell a group of teenagers that sex is holy, we would be met by guffaws of laughter and/or stiffened expectations of a moralistic lecture

And yet, the view of sex as a way to intimacy with other human beings, and into intimacy with the Father, Son and Spirit is a distinctively Catholic view. That is what we mean by listing matrimony as one of our seven sacraments. Sex education, then, is part and parcel of religious education, and the handing on of our sexual values is part of our handing on of our religious beliefs to a new generation. For both of these transmissions the key to success is the same: a high level of sexual intimacy between parents, their continuing cultivation of their passion for each other. In fact, sex education is one basic way in which the sexual intimacy of parents helps children to find their identities. For children cannot acquire an identity that is not sexual. Our sexuality, our being either masculine or feminine, is not like our other traits — a part of our makeup as persons that is somewhat incidental. I can imagine myself, for example, as having been born with blue eyes instead of green, or with a talent for playing the guitar instead of teaching philosophy. But when I try to imagine myself as having been a boy instead of a girl, I am no longer imagining myself. I am imagining some other person. Our sexual identities are central to our identities as persons.

Thus if a child grows up successfully, finds his or her true identity and enjoys it, finding and enjoying his or her sexual identity will be an automatic success also. Likewise, one who is confused, inhibited and unhappy in his or her sexuality will be confused, inhibited and unhappy as a person. Sexual identity and personal identity go together. The passion of parents automatically gives children the most important message about sex that they need to hear: that sex is not just intercourse, but intimacy. It is not just an episodic urgency. Marriage is not just a licensed series of one-night stands, but a continuous passionate presence. The main point of sex, then, is not "What do I get out of it?" but "Whom do I belong to?" Sexual passion, after all, can have tremendously destructive power. It motivates most of the murders we read about in the daily papers, it breaks up families, destroys careers, and ruins reputations. Children are bound to know these facts. But couples who cultivate their desire and come to belong to each other demonstrate to their children, in the only really convincing way, that sex also has a strong positive redemptive power.

Children raised in passionate homes thus almost automatically come to see sex as good, holy, the way for a man and woman to actualize each other's full potential as persons. In the cultivation of their sexual intimacy, parents have then something to put in the place of the "hang-ups" that most of us over forty were raised on. We don't need to sit by helplessly while the pendulum swings to the opposite side. In the present day sex is no longer dirty and sinful, but it can be cheap and trivial. We do have something else to offer. Passionate parents find, and can hand on to their children, a meaning to sexual intimacy that is more exciting than any meaning they might find elsewhere. Passion can give adolescent children an especially deep sense of their own self-worth as sexual beings. The sexual aura in the homes of passionate spouses does not just make open discussion of sex easy and comfortable. It is an atmosphere which makes discussion about the holiness of sex credible, and thus a powerful antidote to the sexual values of our culture.

These secular values were illustrated very well in the 1983 Academy Award winning movie, *Terms of Endearment.* The movie was billed as the story of a life-long relationship between a highly neurotic mother and her daughter, and so it was. But the movie also portrayed several sexual relationships that are quite typical in our culture, even accepted as normal. The marriage of Emma and Flap, the infidelities of both of them, and the liaison between Aurora and Garrett were all relationships based on episodic sexual attraction and nothing more. Each member of each pair went into the relationship with a basically self-centered, "What'sin-this-for-me?" point of view. They had no concern for any love or personal intimacy, no thought of an ongoing presence in each other's minds and hearts. No one even thought about the welfare of the children in the movie. They were just accidental, and incidental, consequences of sex as mere intercourse.

No matter how many popular movies they see, children who live in passionate homes will know better. They will know that sex is something more than an episodically pleasant activity that reinforces our inborn self-centeredness. They will experience, as a daily fact of real life, two people whose sexual desire has led them so far out of themselves that they no longer think of themselves as separate individuals. They will know tenderness and enjoy people simply for being who they are. In a home where sexual intimacy is as evident as cooking odors, they will see our culture for what it is; they will see through its efforts to use sex to sell everything from toothpaste to automobiles. They will not think its main purpose is to entertain, though the inane innuendos popular television shows may seem to indicate the contrary. They will not need sex to give them cheap excitement in a culture where the deeper excitement of real intimacy has gone by the boards. In passionate homes, children will know in their heart of hearts that sex is good for them, too, that their parents' passion for each other is what makes them feel loved and accepted.

But of course, the sexual desire of spouses must not be a secret from their children. Children don't need to observe their parents' lovemaking. But they do need to perceive the aura of passion in their homes, and to know that it is no accident. They need to be told, in a few simple words, that their parents' gentleness towards each other, their acceptance of each other, their joy in each other, is no accident. Nor does it happen automatically with the passage of time. Their sexual desire is the result of a sacramental grace which they have eagerly accepted as a gift of God and given careful nurture throughout their life together.

Ironically, many parents think that it is good to fight openly in front of their children, because such 'honesty' will give the children a 'realistic' picture of married life and human relationships. But few parents feel easy about showing their passion in front of their children. They are uncomfortable in showing any physical signs of affection, and never reminisce about their good times in bed, or anticipate their future sexual contacts. They almost pretend to their children (and sometimes even to each other) that they don't have any sexual contact, or at least any that is worth talking about. (I once caught myself wondering whether it was sinful for spouses to think about sex in between their actual acts of intercourse. The idea was that deeply ingrained in me that sexual thoughts are automatically sinful! I soon came to see, thank God, that all of married life is one long process of making love, that each day's activities are both foreplay and afterplay. Now I can laugh at those early fears. I realize that steady and deliberate sexual fantasizing is an important part of cultivating the intimacy that is our sacramental symbol.) But if children are to learn one of the most important lessons about sex — that it is not episodic and action-oriented, but a constant indwelling in each others' minds and hearts — they must see and hear the affectionate teases and squeezes that keep that presence alive.

Sexual intercourse should have its due privacy, then, but the sexual intimacy which is a couple's way of life is very much their children's business. It is the source of their children's identity, and children have an absolute right to have that intimacy displayed before them in a forthright and exciting fashion. It is their main source of hope for their futures. We must also tell them, in words that they can understand, what it feels like to be close to someone, what are some of the things we do to make each other feel especially loved and cherished, and what we especially delight in about each other.

They need to hear us reminisce about our early romance, to hear the story of how we met and fell in love, what our first date was like, when and how we decided to marry, and so on. We should tell them how we have changed over the years, as a result of our sexual intimacy — how we have become more gentle and understanding, more confident and self-forgetful, less selfish, less afraid of life (and of death). Even sexual failures need not be off limits. What's wrong with telling them that we are a bit grouchy this morning because our lovemaking did not go as well as we had hoped? Or that we're feeling frustration because the whole family's ten-day bout with the flu has kept us from having any relaxed time alone together?

Since this parental intimacy is the source of the children's identities, just as the melting snow in the mountains is the ongoing source of a river, the more evident it becomes to them the more secure they will be about their identities and their own sexuality. Gradually, explanations will become less and less necessary. The children will notice for themselves how free-flowing passion makes their parents tender, relaxed, joyous — and how irritable, harsh, angry parents need to rejuvenate their passion. "Why don't you two take time out and go hold each other for a while?" might be an embarrassing suggestion the first time it comes from one of our children. But once we look beyond that embarrassment, we will be delighted. Any parents who are fortunate enough to hear such a suggestion from one of their children ought to exult in it as they go off to their bedroom. For a little child is leading them, and the fact that the child knows how to do so, and feels free to do so, is a wonderful tribute to their passion.

> I was fortunate enough to have parents that did not think sex was dirty and shameful. They thought it was funny. I heard jokes about sex all my life, and had the impression from the start that it was fun. But I was thirty-five years old before I learned that it can be an expression of love and affection.

Children who do not see the connection between sex and love because their parents' passion is not made abundantly clear to them, may have another problem. They may conclude that, even though sex is fun, love itself is dull, dutiful, and dispassionate. Then they will not be able to believe in the holiness of sex, in its power to save us from sin and death. They will not be excited by the talk they hear about God, about joy as a sign of God's presence.

And here we come to the deepest reason of all why spouses should cultivate their sexual intimacy, and reveal the intimacy to their children: their intimacy is meant to function as a sacrament, to be the medium in which the message of the gospel is preached. This message is, basically, that love and joy are real, that we must trust each other and enjoy life together for, in St. John's words, "God is Love, and he who lives in love, lives in God, and God lives in Him." Sexual intimacy, when it gets that message across, does much more than promote the mental health and maturity of children.

One day a young woman student came to my office for some counselling. She sat down, and said, "I think I should begin by telling you about my religious beliefs." I said, "Fine," and listened carefully:

> 'I used to be a Catholic, but I'm not anymore. I was raised a Catholic. But now I just go to mass on Sunday to please my mother. I don't believe in the Catholic religion anymore. Instead'—and here she became very earnest—'instead, I believe that God is Love. Now, I don't think you can just turn that around and say that love is God. But I do think that when we love, we somehow come close to God, or participate in God, or something like that.'

I just stared at Peggy for a moment, thinking that she was putting me on. Was it possible that she had been raised a Catholic and did not know that she was stating very clearly and accurately the very heart of Catholic belief? But as I pondered a bit, I realized that it was possible. The first letter of St. John was not a part of the regular liturgical readings in those days. And so, it could happen that someone would to to Sunday mass for many years without hearing those words. Peggy's obvious sincerity convinced me that she had, indeed, come to that belief on her own, through a long personal struggle. Her attendance at Sunday mass, along with her mother, had not been much help to her.

This conversation bears out something that Father Andrew Greeley learned a few years ago in one of his sociological surveys. He was curious about what factors are important for keeping children in the church, for having them continue, as adults, the religious beliefs and practices of their childhood. He then surveyed two groups of young adults, married and with families of their own, who had been raised as Catholics by Catholic parents. Those in the first group were still believing, practicing Catholics, while those in the second group were not. The only significant difference between the two groups was parental passion. Those who continued in the religion of their childhood had perceived an atmosphere of passionate sexual intimacy between their parents as they were growing up. Those in the second group, who had abandoned the religion of their childhood, had no such perception: sexual intimacy was either absent from their childhood homes or, for some reason, present but not evident to them. This perception of their parents' passion was what counted. It was a stronger influence than any other factor included in the survey—more important than family prayer, than regular attendance at Sunday mass, and than parochial school education.

This connection between sexual intimacy and the handing on of the faith to a new generation is no accident, nor is it any surprise. It is exactly the way in which a sacrament functions. Sacraments reveal the nature of God, and actually bring His presence into our lives. For anyone who would believe, with Peggy, that "God is Love, and he who lives in love lives in God, and God in him," must believe in the reality of love itself. But believing in the reality of love is not as easy as it sounds. It is not something we do automatically as we go through life. In fact, one of the deepest fears of any human heart is that love is not real, that it is an illusion or an adolescent dream. It is easy to believe that 'real life' consists of more important things. That fear, too, is often reinforced by the human relationships portrayed in our popular music, movies and television programs. Love is something we must not put our hearts into, because it doesn't last. And since it doesn't last, it is never real to begin with. As the song says, "If you love, don't let it show. Don't give yourself away."

When children grow up in a home that is not passionate, their fears about the unreality of love are reinforced every single day. Such children have no experience to counteract what they get from their culture. Where they do not see any love between their parents—love that is throbbingly, passionately real—they easily drift into cynicism and despair. Then they do not believe in the reality of love even when they meet the genuine article. One eighty-year-old woman recently told me, in tears, that of her six children, only one really loves her. I have known this family well for over forty years, and I know that all of this woman's children love her, not just the one. Anyone who knows the family can see that she is constantly breaking their hearts by her refusing to believe in their love and to accept it.

But this woman was brought up in a home where sex was never discussed, where passion was confined to the bedroom, and where the children were given neither information nor values about human sexuality. She became an unwed mother at the age of sixteen, and had three failed marriages. She has now grown old in her inability to believe in the reality of love, even when it is right under her nose. And needless to say, her children, while they love her and know that they do, have many problems in their own marriages and with their own children. The whole family, into the third and even fourth generations, has a kind of joyless attitude that life is an endurance contest, punctuated with moments of joy that are few and far between. They find it very hard to believe in God, the God who is Love.

Parents, then, owe their children the cultivation of their own sexual intimacy. It is as simple as that. Parents who neglect their passion and allow it to cool present a dormant sacrament to their children. They obscure the message of the gospel to their children, and inhibit the influx of grace to them. For if children cannot trust a human love that they *do* see, how will they ever trust the divine love that they *do not* see? But passionate parents reveal to their children in a vivid and credible way the love and joy that circulate among Father, Son and Spirit, in the inner life of God. They proclaim the gospel message loud and clear: the message that all of us are loved passionately and enthusiastically, just for being who we are. Sexual intimacy is one of the clearest places we know of where the medium is, indeed, the message.

CHAPTER SEVEN

Sex Builds The Church

People who know the Roman Catholic Church only from the out-side usually think of her in terms of the Eucharist and sexual morality (especially her stand on contraception, abortion, and homosexuality). But the truth is that matrimony is one of her main features. Most Catholic adults are married, and their way of life is meant to model the intimacy that all people are called to. Spouses are not just each other's helpers. Sexual intimacy is meant for the well-being of the whole Church. Sex builds the Church. That idea is startling at first, because we are so used to having celibates held up as model Christians. But the truth is that all followers of Christ are meant to live in ecstatic, tender love for each other. When celibates become holy, their lives are ecstatic and tender, too. But the celibate way of life is not so evident an ecstasy as that of couples. Moreover, celibate life is the harder way. It is not easy to over-come shame and self-primacy, to be tender and enthusiastic in loving other people, without the energy of genital sex. It is possible of course. But it is not the ordinary way. The passion of ordinary couples is a more common way to transfigure people, and their transfiguration is usually more obvious than that of celibates. Matrimony is a sacrament. Celibacy is not.

Sex, then, is not just one of the kinds of love to be found in the Church. It is the primary kind—the most important, the most evident, the one which literally builds the Church. For what is the Church? Nothing more than a community of those who, in their love for each other, take part in the love play of the Trinity. Couples build that community precisely by being sacraments of such love. What makes a couple be a couple is their intimacy. And what makes the Church be a church is her intimacy. But couples don't just model intimacy—they actually cause it, in their own relationship, in their families, in those who already belong to the Church, and in those who have yet to become her members. Let's see how this happens.

The sacrament of matrimony is not a wedding ritual. It is the passion which a couple bring to their wedding to be ritualized, so that they can live it more deeply, and forever. At their wedding they offer their passion to the Church as a model of loving intimacy for all the world to see. And their offering is a promise — a promise by the couple to nurture their passion, and a promise by the Church to help them to do that. Sexual intimacy is a uniquely powerful model. It draws everyone's attention. When we pass lovers on the street, don't we notice them? Don't we know immediately what they feel for each other? Passionate spouses, then, are not just overwhelmingly attractive to each other. Their love is irresistible and reassuring to everyone who sees it. All the world loves a lover. And that is exactly how a sacrament functions. Sacraments are symbols. They are meant to be noticed, and to draw people toward them.

Passion, then, is one of our great untapped resources for evangelizing. It transforms couples within their individual selves, so that everything they do is changed. Everything they do involves their new identity. A couple's passion is bound to affect their children, their relatives and friends, and anyone else whom they have any contact with. Passionate couples truly proclaim the gospel. They become credible symbols of the God Who is Love. How often have we heard that we owe the Church a share of our money? Sexual desire is part of her patrimony, too. Couples owe it as a contribution to their parishes. For passion is, indeed, one of God's everyday miracles. There is no more powerful sign for calling people's attention to the presence of God in their midst.

Can we imagine what the Church would look like to outsiders if Catholic couples were known for passionate, unrestrained, ecstatic love? Such a picture boggles our minds. Now we can count on a "good Catholic couple" for fidelity to dogmas and rules, for kindness and peace in their home, perhaps for better-than-average verbal communication. But the sparks of passion flash only sporadically, if at all. Restraint is the keynote. But what if these priorities were reversed? What if passion came first, so that as soon as we heard the phrase "a good Catholic couple", we would think of sexual desire, ecstasy, enthusiasm — people crazy about each other and not afraid to let it show? Such passion would be a beacon lighting the way to the Church of Christ. And for those already living as her members, the fire of sexual love would weld deeper, stronger, and more intense bonds of intimacy. For sacraments are not just symbols. They cause what they symbolize. How does the energy of passion build the Church? Let's take an example:

Eloise grew up in a very unhappy home. Her parents argued constantly. Her father drank a lot, and couldn't hold a job. When he tried to touch his wife affectionately, she pushed him aside and said, "Keep your dirty hands off of me." When Eloise was 15, her father simply disappeared, and she never saw him again. One day, when she was away at college, Eloise went with one of her roommates to a friend's home to visit. The friend was a young doctor with a pretty wife and five young children. As soon as she stepped through the door, Eloise saw that here was a happy home. The couple were quite obviously in love with each other, and were delighted with their children. Eloise burst into tears at the sight of their happiness. That visit gave her hope, for the first time in her life, that she might someday have a happy marriage and family, too. And later on she did.

Now, if a sociologist heard this story he would see in it the strength of the family, the basic unit of society. A psychologist might point out how a happy, loving childhood helps children grow up with better mental and emotional health. And these experts would be right. But they would miss the most important point: Bob and Mary Jane, the happy couple whom Eloise visited, were able to radiate love in such a powerful way because of their passion for each other. It was their sexual intimacy which welcomed their children. Their sexual intimacy made the atmosphere of their home so happy that it was evident to a stranger the moment she stepped in the door. Bob and Mary Jane, in other words, were a sacrament. The power of their passion certainly transformed the two of them. But it also had ripple effects, like a pebble thrown into a pond. In creating their passionate intimacy, they showed everyone — their children, their friends, and Eloise and other strangers — the reality of human love. They made that reality so shiningly clear that no one could doubt it. And in that symbol, they made God credible, too.

St. John caught this power of the sacrament of sexual intimacy in the few simple words we have quoted before: "God is love, and he who lives in love, lives in God, and God in Him." Eloise eventually came to know and to love the family she visited, and so came into the circle of their love. The circle of their love expanded to include her. If Eloise had not met them, or some other intimate couple, when she did, her childhood fears might have lasted throughout her adult life. And if love — human love — had never been made credible to her, divine love would not have been believable either. As it turned out she became a believing Catholic, and has remained so, thanks to the witness of such couples as Bob and Mary Jane.

St. Augustine knew about this ripple effect of love, especially of sexual love. He wondered why incest should be forbidden, as it is in all known human societies. Sexual intercourse is such a powerful and natural way to express our strongest love and affection that it would seem right for family members to make love to each other. And yet we do not. And St. Augustine tells us why: sexual intercourse is meant to widen the circle of love. If we exercised that most powerful language within our families, we would never look outside them for someone to love. Then love would not become sacramental, a beacon guiding outsiders to the Church. Love would stay closed in the tight little circle of each family. And then the Church would not come to be. Therefore, we all have to marry strangers. We cannot marry someone from the family in which we were born and raised. But as we go out of our families and seek strangers to marry, those strangers eventually come to be even more intimate to us than our original family members. And so, the circle of love is extended. For a marriage is not just the joining of two individuals. It is the joining of two families. After a wedding has joined two families, the members of both usually look outside that wider circle to find their partners, and as new strangers come into the web of family intimacy, their families come into it, too. I am not just forbidden to marry those to whom I am related by blood, but also some of those to whom my blood relatives are related by marriage. And so, as the circle of love becomes wider and wider, the Church — *the* circle of those who love — comes into being, all as a result of the passion that draws two strangers to become each other's sexual intimates.

One day my telephone rang. It was Louise, who was disposing of some furniture she no longer needed. "Mary," she said, "I have my grandmother's bed here, and can't use it anymore. But I would like to keep it in the family. None of my children have space for it, either. I was wondering if you would like to have it for Eddie?" Of course I was delighted to accept the bed, on behalf of my infant son. But I was more delighted to accept the love which Louise offered in such a simple, matter-of-fact way. You see, Louise had no blood ties to my son — only the ties of love. Her sister is the wife of the man whose late sister was my husband's first wife. And Eddie is our adopted son. And yet, to Louise, giving her grandmother's bed to Eddie was a way of keeping it in the family! There is a perfect example of how passion widens the circle of love. Grandma and grandpa had been total strangers. But one day they fell in love, married, and bought a double bed. In that bed they begot their children and, as their passion lasted through the years, they guided those children in the ways of love. Their daughters grew up and fell in love, too. Their passion widened the circle of love to include their spouses, and their spouses' families. The love was so strong that when Mary Carol died, her husband was still considered very much a member of the family. Later, I, his second wife, and then our adopted children, were also welcomed into the family. And that is how Louise could, in a simple matter-of-fact way, offer her grandmother's bed to Eddie as a way of keeping it in the family. Had passion died and marriages broken up, Eddie would never have become a member of that family. Had passion even cooled, so that children and grandchildren did not learn to love, he would not have been included either.

Blood ties are important, of course, and so is the sheer biological production of children. But biology does not make a family, and it does not make a Church either. Only love can do that. And the most powerful way to produce love and make it grow is through the sexual passion of sacramental couples. Louise's grandparents did not just love each other. They did so with a passion that made love credible and attractive to their children and grandchildren. There are many groups of people who hold together because they love each other. But the Church is the only circle of love that is sacramental. All of us human beings are born knowing absolutely nothing about human life, not even whether it is worth living or not. We learn about life from the people we associate with, particularly our families. If we are to be living, breathing members of the Church of Christ (which I like to call the First Trinitarian Church), we have to come to believe in the reality of love. We have to really believe, deeply enough to stake our lives on it, that love is real, not just a sentimental, adolescent dream that we must give up in order to grow up. In fact, we must believe that love is the most real thing there is—more so than money, food, air, or any of the things we see and feel and hear. For, as St. John tells us, God is Love. And God is the realest of the real, the Supreme Being. But St. John also tells us about the role of human love in making it possible for us to believe in God. 'How can they love the God Whom they do not see," he asks, "if they do not love the neighbor that they do see?" (I Jn. 4:20).

That is precisely how matrimony, with sex at the heart of it, builds the Church. We have many examples of love in our world. Public figures such as Pope John Paul II and Mother Theresa of Calcutta shine before all the world, and there are countless others whom no one hears of. Devoted social workers and parish priests, mothers in neighborhoods, concerned teachers and doctors, youth workers, grocery clerks—all can and do provide examples of love at work in everyday life. And some of these examples do help us to believe in the reality of love. But the passion of sacramental couples does more. First of all, sexual passion is dramatic. It gets people's attention right away. Aren't we struck by couples who have been married a long time and are still obviously in love with each other? "Oh, oh! Here come the lovebirds." Such couples are doing exactly what they ought to do — being sacramental by letting their love show. People who know them know that love is real because they experience it.

But sacramental couples do much more than give examples of love. Sacraments, remember, are not just symbols — they also cause what they symbolize. Passionate couples, then, not only show the rest of us where the God who is love is present. They actually make Him present, in and through their love. And it is our common sharing in the presence of Divine Love that makes us a Church. Passionate couples, who become transformed from being strangers into being intimates, help all the rest of us strangers become each other's intimates, too. They do so by making Love credible, so that we can believe in it. And once we believe, we can begin to live it. Then all of us strangers begin to be each other's intimates. And then we are the Church.

The aura of tenderness that sexual passion generates is very important, then, for building the Church. Couples who have been transfigured, changed into tender and joyous spouses, have left suspicion, jealousy, fear of intimacy (all the sins of individualism) behind in their life with each other. And since they have done that, they draw other people out of their individualism, too. Passionate spouses do not need to control or manipulate each other, because they do not need to protect themselves from the fear that love is not really real. They feel the reality of love in their bones. But that tenderizing of their hearts towards each other affects the way they act toward other people, too, beginning with their children, then moving out to the rest of their family, to the people they work with, and finally to everyone they meet. The way in which passion widens the circle of love is so ordinary that we might not even notice it. But it is one of God's miracles, one of His sacraments. Passionate people are more relaxed and accepting toward everyone they meet. And so, the people they meet also relax and accept others, because they feel accepted, trusted, and affirmed, rather than used and manipulated.

One day in the waiting room of my pediatrician's office, a black mother was downright cruel to her five-year-old daughter. The girl was whimpering a bit because her mother would not let her sit in an empty chair across the room, next to her two brothers. The mother insisted that the girl stand close to her. Suddenly the mother took the girl out into the corridor and spanked her really hard for her whimpering. As she spanked her, she said, "You are nobody, do you understand that? There are important people who need to sit in that chair."

I spoke up for the little girl. "You shouldn't tell her she's nobody," I protested. "She is a beautiful little girl."

The mother gave me a scornful look, and said, "Well, if you think you can raise her better than I'm doing, you're welcome to her. She ain't no good to me."

The mother's anger so upset me that I had to leave the room to compose myself. As I did, a black father, who was there with two of his children, tried to comfort me. "I understand how you feel," he said, "and I agree with you. But they ain't no use gettin' upset. That's just every-day life." What had upset me, of course, was the realization that this was, indeed, everyday life. The mother was not in a momentary fit of anger. She wasn't out of control. She was quite calm and methodical, and it was evident to me that this was her usual way of treating her daughter.

I mention this incident, and point out that the people involved were black, in order to show something about passion in sacramental mar-riages. You don't have to be a trained psychologist to see that this mother had problems of her own. She was acting out her feelings that she, herself, was nobody. Possibly she was a single parent. But the fact that she was black told me something: every day of her life she had had to hear racial insults and to live with the pain of knowing that her children would do the same. If our American society were saturated with passionate couples, such racism would not exist. People who, in their passion for each other, have become convinced of the reality of human love, and of our con-stant living in the Love of the Three Divine Persons, would not have racist feelings and certainly would not take part in the discrimination against minorities that is so large a feature of our society. Certainly many of the problems experienced in black families, including the one which I experienced so dramatically in my doctor's office, would never happen if black children received the same education as white children, if black men had the same job opportunities, if black parents did not have to teach their children from their earliest years how to absorb countless daily insults without becoming bitter, angry adults. Certainly the healing of racial prejudices in white families would be a large step toward the heal-ing of broken and hurting black families.

The healing would come about through the same psychological process that we described above, the building of the Church through the widening of the circle of love. Since Vatican II, we hear a great deal about making the Church relevant to our times, of bringing the gospel home to the real lives of real people. We hear — and rightly so — about the need to bring about social justice, to eliminate poverty and hunger, to treat minorities with dignity, to abolish the arms race, and to give women their rights. With the need for social justice so great, it may seem naive and utopian, even a way of avoiding problems, to talk about a need for more passionate couples. It might seem that social needs are more urgent and that the luxury of sexual intimacy should take second place. But the sexual intimacy we are calling for is not a luxury that the world can dispense with. We are not talking about couples billing and cooing in a corner while the world goes to destruction all around them. Social justice is certainly all important. If we neglect that, we simply deny the gospel. But the passion that we are advocating for couples, nourished by SSPT, is not a distraction to social justice efforts, or a substitute for them. It is their ground and foundation.

Social problems are simply the mistreatment of individuals on a grand scale. To take racism as an example, people look down on those who have a different color of skin out of a need to make themselves feel good. One way to build up our own self-esteem is to look down on others, to think that we are better than they. People who enjoy sexual intimacy cannot be racists. It is psychologically impossible to them. For when a couple cultivate their sexual passion, they find themselves strengthened every day by sexual touches. Now the sense of touch is our most powerful indicator of what is real and what is not. The right kind of sexual touching, and intercourse in particular, convinces us more strongly than anything else that we are loved and cherished, that we can love and cherish someone else. Isn't it a powerful reassurance that people care about us when they touch us in some way? When we are sick, we know at once which of the doctors and nurses taking care of us also care about us. We know by the way they touch — or don't touch.

The sense of touch plays the same powerful role in the building of sexual intimacy, and the transfiguration of spouses. Men and women who enjoy such intimacy have no doubts about their own self-worth. They feel it in their bones. They have no doubts that love is real and that life is good when people love each other. They have no doubts about their own ability to love and they exercise that love wherever they go. And so a sacramental wife or husband simply finds racism unthinkable. They cherish every human being, and do not judge people on the color of their skin. They do not need to look down on someone else in order to feel good about themselves.

I had my purse snatched by a black teenager recently. And I must confess, for months afterwards I felt uneasy whenever I saw black teenagers coming toward me on the street. But that fear was foolish and a sign that I am not yet perfect in my marital intimacy. After all, if a white juvenile had snatched my purse, I wouldn't have felt the same fear of other white teenagers. True, statistics show that there is more delinquency among blacks than among whites — twice as much, in fact. But look at these statistics: about 5% of white teenagers are delinquents, and 10% of blacks. That means that nine out of ten black teenagers are just fine. I have no reason to fear all of them as I meet them on the street. But I do fear them, because I still have some remnants in me of the racism of my society, of the family and the culture that I was raised in. God, working in and through my passion for my husband, is not finished with me yet.

When we emphasize sex as the way to build the Church, then, we are not suggesting a "benign neglect" of social problems. We simply must do everything we can to see that every human being on the face of God's green earth — His big blue marble — has enough food, water and shelter, education and medical care, civil rights and dignity, to live the life of love. We are, though, saying that sex is a powerful way to bring about social justice because it widens the circle of love. After all, justice is not what the Church is about. Love is. We are not just to feed the hungry. We are to love them, to invite them into the intimacy which is the Church. People who have the finest food and clothing, fancy homes, sophisticated medical care, social and political freedom and financial security but do not live in loving intimacy with their fellows are missing the point of their lives. We must, then, invite the poor and the oppressed into full intimacy with the rest of us. We must, of course, care for their material needs. But that caring is a means to an end, that of intimacy.

It is one thing to offer material help at a distance — though that is better than not offering it at all. But the gospel asks us to love the people we help, to invite them to intimacy as our equals. That invitation takes a lot of courage, a solid self-esteem, a deep trust in the reality of God's love. Spouses who are transformed into confident, trusting, loving persons are our best bet to be such missionaries. And meanwhile, developing sexual intimacy among oppressed couples themselves will be an enormous gift. Our social problems are simply staggering. When we think of the kind of change we need to make — social change, change on a grand scale, through law and other institutions — we can easily despair. Certainly such change is not going to come about in a single generation, even if we make our best effort. Meanwhile, there is some real hope, some unique hope, that we can offer to oppressed people of our own time: sexual intimacy in their own marriages.

Victor Frankl saw, in Hitler's death-camps, that people who had loving relationships with each other were able to survive, to tolerate the worst forms of physical and psychological suffering. Those who did not belong to some kind of loving network soon gave up. They saw no meaning in life, no reason to go on. There is a lesson here for all of us. Intimacy creates a basic joy in life that nothing can take away. If, then, we offered to the minorities and poor of our own country as well as oppressed people all over the world the chance to enjoy sacramental sex, to nurture passion in their marriages, we would give them a powerful tool for survival. We would give them a gift of joy in spite of their suffering, something that would make their lives well worth living while they wait for the social changes that will correct the poverty, racism, and militarism that presently scar their lives.

And then we would see a new widening of the circle of love. For when we heighten the sexual passion of poor and oppressed couples, we make the good news relevant to their daily lives in a most powerful way. Their heightened passion will become sacramental, too. We mustn't give up our efforts toward social justice then. However, the poor may have something to teach the rest of us. When people have nothing in life except each other, they sometimes develop strength, sensitivities and loyalties to each other that are quite remarkable. Those strengths can become sacramental if we welcome them into the Church and celebrate the passion that is their root.

In fact, we can think of no better way to relieve the many hostilities in our society than through the sexual passion of sacramental couples. Sex gentles people and tenderizes their hearts. It affects people in the deepest roots of their personalities — the ability to trust, to love, to give up defenses and become vulnerable. We don't mean, of course, that couples and others who try to love are expecting to get hurt, or even looking for pain in some masochistic way. Rather, we hope that sexual intimacy will minimize hurts, and heal those that do occur. But we have to be vulnerable, and open to the possibility of being hurt, because the only other way is to be defensive. Defensive people are tough, self-sufficient, isolated, and self-centered. This difference showed up in a recent conversation I overheard. Mildred, mother of two teenagers, was talking to her own mother, Kate, about how to raise children:

"I think you are doing it all wrong, Mildred. You give your children too much praise and affection. Nobody in the world out there is going to care about their feelings, or their self-esteem. And you shouldn't either. You should make them tough for the world they will have to face when they grow up."

"Well," said Mildred — choking back tears because her mother's words brought back instant memories of many painful hurts she had felt as a child — "I disagree with you on that. I think the most important thing family members should do for each other is care about each other's feelings, and build each other's self-esteem."

"Well," said Kate, "that isn't the way I was brought up."

What Kate said was perfectly true. She was raised in an immigrant family in which all matters of sex were hushed up, affection was restrained, and the children were made to feel inferior to their native-born American friends. Kate had to leave school in eighth grade to go to work at home. She became an unwed mother in her teens, had several failed marriages, and raised six children whose lives also had many problems. Mildred, one of those six children, had found healing for her childhood hurts in the passion of her own marriage, and was raising her children in a different way. But it took her many years to overcome her childhood. She had grown up basically suspicious of people, unable to trust them, and very lonely. Her husband's passion for her, and hers for him, gradually changed her. She is now more relaxed and open, and is trying to raise her own children to be the same way.

The family, so goes the cliché, is the basic unit of society. And so it is. It is the basic unit of the Church, too. When homes are peaceful and happy, society is, too, and so are parishes. The reason is not hard to see. Our homes, more than any other factor, determine what kinds of persons we are. Our homes make us either manipulative, insecure seekers of our own individual happiness, or self-forgetful, ecstatic, self-abandoning intimates. Since these identities go with us wherever we go, the atmosphere of our homes affects an ever-widening circle of other people. People often think that praise and affection lead us to become conceited and self-centered, to get "big heads". But the truth is just the opposite. When we receive praise and affection from those around us, our security about our self-worth leads us to relax and forget about ourselves, to enjoy other people and care about them. And that is what makes intimacy possible. The key, though, is the passion of spouses. For when spouses praise each other, and live in evident desire for each other, praise and affection flow like wine. The wine overflows, automatically, to everyone they meet or have any dealings with. It is criticism that makes us self-centered, that leads us to an anxious preoccupation with our own self-worth, that causes us to use people for our own security, seeking their approval from behind defensive masks.

We don't have to be experts in social psychology to know that aggressive and hostile people, those who commit violent crimes and abuse their spouses and children, are often acting out their sexual frustrations. Their own sexual lives need healing. But sex goes much deeper than that.

We are sexual beings through and through. This is true whether we are "sexually active" or not, whether we are married or celibate. And married people are not just sexual in their relationship with each other. We are all sexual in all of our interactions with all people. Our very selves are sexual. That is why sexual insults are so powerful. When we are angry with someone, and want to speak the foulest insult we can think of, we say something sexual — even if the issue that we are angry about has nothing to do with sex. What do we call people who take our parking space, or hold political views that we don't agree with? That's right — we make slurs about their mothers' sexual behavior! Such insults are devastating because our sexuality is central to our very identities as persons. If I fail as a woman, I fail as a person, because that is the kind of person I am. And if I fail as a person, I fail completely. And if a man is deficient in his virility, or has problems relating with women, he feels deficient as a person, and thus feels deficient in a total way. Sexual insults hurt because they insult our very persons. And sexual healing is also a healing of total persons.

Here, again, we see what is special about sex, about the intimacy between passionate, devoted spouses. It symbolizes and reveals totality in an especially clear way. All love is total. That is, if we truly love anyone, even a stranger, we are willing to give up our life for that person. But spouses do give up their lives for each other, all day, every day. They abandon their total selves to each other in intercourse. And they share more of the details of everyday life, and more memories and hopes, than people do in any other relationship. Such totality is a promise, though, to everyone else. It is the spouses' way of announcing to the world that they wish to love everyone, that they wish to share Trinitarian life to the maximum with everyone they meet. Of course we live with different degrees of intimacy with various people. We may say just a casual "Good morning" to the bus driver, and later in the day help a grieving family express their feelings. But sex provides the model for all these lesser intimacies.

Sex does more than that. When we love, we love with our feelings. And these are conditioned by our own sexuality. And that sexuality is largely the product of our formative years, our early childhood and adolescence. Our ability to love as adults, then, depends a great deal on the quality of passion that our parents enjoyed. Many women are unhappy as adults because of unsolved problems that they had with their mothers. Chances are that those problems were problems which the parents had with each other. The staff psychiatrist at Marquette University Counseling center put it well: "We assume that when you have a troubled adolescent, you've got a troubled marriage in the background.

It's very nearly 100% true." And, of course, the parents' problems could very likely be traced to deficiencies in their parents' sexual intimacy, and so on, back into the mists of time. Psychiatrists once thought that mental illness was hereditary because the same problems seem to crop up in one generation after another in families. Now, most of them are more inclined to think that problems repeat themselves because we raise our children the way we were raised, and they will raise theirs pretty much the same way. A new generation does not start from scratch, but takes on, at birth, the luggage of many generations. The passion of an intimate couple goes on and on, through the generations. And so do the inhibitions of a dispassionate couple.

When we say, then, that hostile and aggressive people are often acting out sexual frustrations, we do not mean that they need intercourse more often, or need to find greater satisfaction in their own sexual relations. That may or may not be true. What we can be sure of is that the sexual intimacy of others, mainly their parents, has influenced them in the past, and is influencing them now. And the same is true for people who live in easy, self-forgetful enjoyment of other people. For the way that adults live together reflects, in most cases, what they experienced as children. The effects of passion don't stop at the bedroom door. They pour out into the rest of the house and the rest of the world, into school, church, office and marketplace. The power of the sacrament of matrimony to build the Church is literally boundless. Whether or not the Church herself functions as a credible symbol of God's love, drawing people to Him, depends directly on the credibility of her married couples. For people most often form their opinion of the Church from their impression of the Catholics they know. And most Catholics are married.

Some parishes stand out for being progressive in their liturgy, others for being oriented toward social justice. But what if a parish were outstanding for the passion of its couples? If Catholics were known everywhere for sexual intimacy, the Church would certainly not look like just one organization among many. She would be a true light in the darkness of ordinary lives. Her light would so shine before men that people who never heard a professional missionary would be drawn to her—for the right reason. Converts haven't flocked to us because of our moral righteousness or our organizational genius. (One convert-friend of mine keeps saying, "It's got to be a divine institution. If it wasn't, it never would have survived its members the way it has.") But converts certainly would flock to us if we showed, in action, the deeply incarnational truth that human sexuality is a genuine and powerful way to holiness. When we say that sex is not evil, that it is quite permissible in certain circumstances, we take but one very tiny step in the right direction. We need to proclaim from the housetops that sex is holy. The passion of couples is part of the Church's inheritance, a pearl of great price, a light that should not be hidden under a bushel. It is a charism which, like other charisms, is for the good of the whole Church. And that good includes her growth through attracting adult converts.

"Let's not knock the Baltimore Catechism. After all, that's what got me into the Church," I said.

"Yes, but don't forget—you were exactly thirteen years old at the time."

My husband's remark was a wise one. I had been reflecting on my life and the ways in which people do come into the Church. I became acquainted with the Church at a very unhappy, chaotic time of my life, after losing both parents in the space of five years (one by suicide, the other by simple desertion). I fell in love with the logic of the catechism. Soon after that, I had a high school course in apologetics, which I also loved. All that logic! It was one syllogism after another. First you prove the existence of God, then you prove the divinity of Christ, then you prove that He founded the Catholic Church, and then you're home free—everything the Church teaches is true because she is the Church of Christ.

That is a simplified view of my conversion, even bordering on a caricature, but it has a grain of truth. Logic and good sense were important in the turmoil of my life, and I welcomed the catechism for that. But the logic soon broke down. A few years later, one of my college professors, a wise and holy Jesuit priest, had me read the works of St. Teresa and St. John of the Cross. I found those books profoundly upsetting, mainly because the two saints let God be so real to them. I didn't want God to be that real to me. I remember saying to myself, in tears, "If that's what it is to be a saint, then I don't want to be a saint."

What had frightened me, of course, was the reality of love. To believe in love that deeply and joyously seemed to me to be a trap to let myself in for terrible heartbreaks and disappointments. And so I set the mystics aside and gave my attention to other things. I wanted to be married and have a family, and somehow vaguely trusted, and hoped, that God would save me in that way. And it is only now, in late middle age, that I can read the mystics with some measure of peace. I still don't love very well, or pray very well, but at least I see what they are talking about. And it is significant that the mystics all use the language of sexual intimacy to express the inexpressible—their experience of God in the higher states of prayer. Passion simply says things that cannot be said in any other way. It enables us to trust the awesome reality of divine Love.

Logic, dogma, systematic theology may have a certain role, even an important one, in drawing some people to the Church. But that role is not primary. No, what enables people to believe in the God Who is Love is just what St. John said. It is love, human love, which makes divine love credible. As I look back over my years in the church, I realize that what enabled me to follow the logic, to believe the dogmas, and to study the theology is the people in my life who have made all of that credible. They are the people who have shown me what it is to love and be loved. And most of them have been married people. Some have been celibates; but all of the credible celibates I have known have understood marital intimacy very well—better than most married people, I would say. And so, the sacrament of matrimony has been operating through them, too. For the Church can be credible in only one way—as a community of intimates, of lovers whose love takes part in the love of Father, Son and Spirit for each other. Sometimes, indeed, the whole message does seem incredible to me (probably because it seems too good to be true). To participate in the very life of God! To be really saved from sin and death! To expect people to belong to each other totally, in an intimacy whose joy is beyond words! To live a whole life of loving and being loved, a life that lasts forever!

When I find my faith in these astounding truths beginning to waver, it is not to logic that I turn, but to people. I look to people who dare to love and be loved, to belong to each other in ecstatic joy. In them I see the Church as *the* answer to *the* question of human life. Her words are important of course, but her people are more so. They are her body language, the language of love *par excellence*. It is hard to imagine how people might come to such love without the example of passionate couples. Indeed, it is hard to imagine how couples would come to such love without passion. In a world without sexual desire, would anyone get excited enough about anyone else to hand himself over, lock, stock, and barrel, for life? Would anyone find joy in doing so? Would intimacy ever happen? Perhaps a few celibates might show us the way to ecstatic self-abandon, as a whole way of life, even as a few do now. But wouldn't we think they were unusual, that their way was for an exceptional few? After all, millions of people admire Mother Teresa. But few feel an urge to join her.

Now imagine another world, one in which Catholic couples were noted for their passion and intimacy, a passion which transfigured them into symbols of the Living Flame of Divine Love. The gospel would seem relevant to everyday life, because it would be relevant. People would fall all over themselves to join such a Church. Few people who know of Jesus question His goodness. What many do question, though, is His relevance to them and their daily lives. Sexual love is central to the lives of most people, but what they usually hear from the Church are prohibitions and inhibitions on sexual love. And so their enthusiasm for the rest of her message is chilled. But if we who know the power of sex to tenderize hearts would celebrate that gift, the gospel would be relevant indeed. People would be drawn to the Church like flies to honey. For who, in all the world, is more attractive than lovers? Whom do we enjoy more, want to be around, want to be like, than those who love and are loved, who are glad to be alive and to share life with everyone they meet?

Enthusiasm has a bad name in some Catholic circles, and certainly it can be an empty or even dangerous emotion. But the root meaning of the word is the same as one of the Bible's names for God — Immanuel. Both terms mean "God is within us." What better way to symbolize that presence than by enthusiasm itself? When enthusiasm is sacramental, as it is in marital intimacy, it does not just symbolize the presence of God. It makes that presence happen. The infectious joy that passionate couples exude — "All the world loves a lover" — is the force that builds the Church. When lovers are present, especially married lovers, people notice, are glad, and feel compelled to respond somehow. And that is precisely how a sacrament functions. It causes people to notice, to rejoice, to respond, to "come and do likewise". The wonder is that such power is found in plain, old garden-variety sexual passion.

That is how sex builds the Church. When we celebrate the sacrament of matrimony, we cease to be *people*. We become, instead, what we call ourselves in the third Eucharistic Prayer — *a* people. Couples bring enthusiasm to the Church and, as they do, fulfill Jesus's prayer at the Last Supper:

> May they all be one.
> Father, may they be one in us,
> so that the world may believe it was you who sent me.
> I have given them the glory you gave to me,
> that they may be one as we are one.
> With me in them and you in me,
> may they be so completely one
> that the world will realize that it was you who sent me
> and that I have loved them as much as you loved me.
>
> (Jn. 17:21-23)

CHAPTER EIGHT

Sex Is A Real Ideal

> Say, are you two really serious? Do you think people are actually going to read a book about intimacy and take it to heart? The average couple can't even think about that. She's too busy with the kids. And he's struggling to stay away from prostitutes when he goes on the road. Get with it—this just isn't real life.

The person who made this comment is a good friend, a respected colleague, a happily married man with a family. His objection made us stop and think. Another friend-philosopher-husband-father said, "Don't be so utopian—the best is the enemy of the good." Have we, then, offered a vision of sex that is naive and unrealistic? Is our ideal so high that couples will be discouraged and not even give it a try? If so, marriages will not become more sacramental. They will not draw people to God by revealing the reality of His Love. Couples will be humdrum, dispassionate, mediocre. No one will notice them or wonder "what makes them tick". No one will connect sex with holiness, or relate married life to intimacy with God.

This "utopian" objection to seeing sex as holy is a serious one. But it is based on a false idea. We don't picture couples living in a state of constant sexual excitement, with devotion that never flags. We do not expect Skin-to-Skin Prime Time to be an instant success. Nor do we expect couples by the dozens to succeed every time they try passionate and tender lovemaking, bringing each other full satisfaction through perfect timing and clear feedback. We are not picturing spouses who enjoy totally clear, open, and honest conversation all day, every day. Nor do we picture them living in perfect understanding and devotion toward their children and other relatives, their friends and acquaintances, their bus drivers and store clerks, and everyone else they meet all day. We don't think of sacramental couples as having a constant and lively sense of intimacy with Father, Son and Spirit. They are not immune to confusion and misunderstandings, to sexual failures, to fatigue, to illness, to petty and grandiose selfishness. Their prayer is not always exuberant. The strength that they draw from the Eucharist is not always evident to those who know them, or even to the couples themselves. Such an ideal would be utopia, indeed. It would be romantic, and thus hopeless.

If this utopian objection is true, we have offered guidance to couples which will mislead them in the most important business of their lives — their eternal salvation. Where we had meant to encourage couples, and excite them, we will have discouraged them, led them to fear and depression. A hopelessly romantic ideal that is false and misleading does more harm than good. In fact, we considered this problem ourselves when we began our book. Anyone who teaches the Christian ideal of life must do so in fear and trembling, even when he speaks to people who are basically good. For the Christian message is awesome, indeed. We who teach it believe that there is meaning to life, and that life is well worth living, no matter what suffering and misery it may bring. We even believe that death itself does not rob life of its meaning, but is instead a transition to fuller, happier, more meaningful life. We believe that there really is healing for the deep self-primacy of human hearts, and that the healing brings a joy beyond anything we can imagine or ask for. What could be more astonishing? We cannot imagine a greater hope, a higher ideal, than what our faith offers to ordinary people. And yet. . .

Isn't it astonishing to say that the meaning of life is in love? People do find deep joy in loving and being loved — at least, some people do, some of the time. But we are saying something much more startling than that. We believe that in loving we all find the solution to our deepest and most serious problem. This problem is our tendency to be our own worst enemies, to do the things that defeat our own happiness. In the saying made popular many years ago by Pogo, "We have met the enemy, and he is us." But we do not despair, even when we see ourselves defeating our own happiness by acting out our self-primacy. We have a real hope that in trying to love we will find our self-destructive tendencies healed. And we will find a joy that never ends, not even when we die. What could be more awesome? The only belief that is more awesome, because it makes this belief in love more concrete, is the belief that sex is holy. We do not offer this vision lightly, but with a full awareness of its weight: for the vast majority of the human race, sexual love spells salvation from sin and death.

There is another reason, though, for people to wonder if we are serious. It is precisely in love — in loving and in being loved, in trying

to love and in hoping to be loved — that we experience our deepest disappointments and our most wretched failures. The overall record of the
human race, if we look at history, has been pretty disappointing: wars,
exploitation, slavery, deceit, competition. And we all know that in our
lives our efforts to give and receive love fall far short from what we would
like them to be. A student said to me one day, "Prof, you are absolutely
right about altruistic love. I've been trying it for three weeks now, and
it really works." He was naive, of course, scarcely realizing how demanding love can be. Moreover, he was finding people responsive when he
reached out to them. But he will find, as he matures, that love does not
always bring a loving response and that, as the banners say, "Love is the
hardest work in the world."

Sometimes it seems, then, that offering people the Christian ideal
of love, and of the holiness of sex, can be a cruel deception. Hoping in
that ideal can lead to big disappointments and failures. Is this vision of
sacramental sex, then, not just unrealistic, but a hoax? Are we offering
such a high hope to couples that it is sure to be smashed on the rocks
of everyday human life? Is it wrong to offer passion and devotion as the
order of the day, to tell people with confidence that they can love as Jesus
did? And that in so loving, they can share in His very life, a life of eternal intimacy with God? Is it even more wrong to hold up the ideal of
sex as a sacramental symbol? For when we do that, we do something
more astounding still. We harness ourselves to an ideal of love that is
already difficult, the most delicate, the most powerful, the most confusing
of human emotions: sexual desire. It is almost as if we commissioned
an artist to make a statue for us, and gave the commission to one who
had no special talent. And on top of that, we gave him very ordinary
materials and asked for a most complex and delicate design. How realistic
is it to think of couples, on a grand scale, achieving the intimacy that
we have proposed? Is our vision just a nice theory? Or does it have some
practical value? Can it really hit you, our readers, where you live?

My husband of nearly thirty years gave us the answer. When we
asked him, "Do you think we will be laughed out of court? Will people
think we are naive and irrelevant?" he answered, "Yes, I think that will
happen. But you should go ahead anyway, because there isn't any alter-
native. This is the only true ideal for the sacrament of matrimony." And
so we have gone ahead. We speak out of faith, convinced that this idea
is true. We also speak out of a realistic hope that this ideal can become
real for thousands of ordinary couples. And we speak out of love for you,
our readers. In our love, we see sexual intimacy not as the work of human
effort alone, but of the Holy Spirit. And when it happens — when our

readers find a new and deeper sexual intimacy in their marriages—we will joyfully take that intimacy as our own. We will rejoice in a new intimacy among us all, readers and authors, and all of us together in the love play of God, of Father, Son and Spirit.

Our invitation to couples to cultivate their passion as the way to eternal life is, then, totally practical and realistic. For nothing is more practical, nothing more realistic, than Jesus' command to love each other as He has loved us. There is no task more hopeful and practical then the task of keeping His commandments, so that He, His Father, and His Spirit, can come to live in us. There is nothing more relevant to the daily lives of ordinary people than the fact that God is Three-in-One, and that His grace and Power are what save us. The artist who creates intimate couples out of ordinary human beings is the Holy Spirit Himself, whose creative talent we can trust completely. Sacramental sex, then, far from being utopian (literally, "nowhere"), is precisely "where it is at". The harnessing of sexual desire to devoted love, delicate, powerful, and confusing as it may seem, is a totally realistic project for ordinary human beings. Couples don't need any special gifts of intelligence, wisdom, or psychological skill, but only the basic faith, hope, and charity of true believers.

We think of sex, then, in much the same way that Churchill thought of democracy. He said, "It is the worst form of government that there is, except for all the others that have been tried." The Church's vision of marriage as sacramental is the most difficult vision of marriage there is—except for all the others. For no other vision of sexual intimacy roots it so deeply in the divine power. Sex is a grace, "the love of God poured forth in our hearts". If sex depended on human efforts, we would despair indeed. But it does not.

It will help, though, if we look more closely at the way in which ideals function in our lives. The dictionary gives two meanings for the word *ideal*: an ideal can be an abstraction or dream which can never be real, or it can be a goal or purpose which guides our action so that we do make it real. The ideal of sex as we first described it above, as perfect, effortless passion, is the first kind of ideal. It is a pipe dream, an illusion, to think of sacramental sex as a state of constant bliss, perfect intimacy, total devotion, and uninterrupted passionate ecstasy beginning on day one of a couple's romance. Such a dream is unrealistic, and no one should hope for it, work for it, or expect it. That ideal is like the dreams of a young boy who pictures himself as a big league pitcher hurling a perfect game every time he takes the mound. Such romantic ideals are naive and out of touch with real people and the real world. The ideal of perfect, effortless, dreamy intimacy leaves out the dark side of human love. The Church certainly knows this dark side, for it is our failures in love that required the death of Jesus to redeem us. And our own experience shows us that couples who try their best to live in passionate devotion often find themselves, to their dismay, acting selfishly. The shame and self-primacy which mar sexual intimacy crop up in the most delicate moments of making love, as well as in countless other situations of our lives together.

> Remember how we used to sit so close together in the front seat, and held hands every time we got a chance? How come we don't do that any more?

> Yes, sure, I remember. Who moved?

Even in the very best marriages, passion often cools. The most passionate, devoted, the most sexual of couples are often distracted and confused, defensive and withdrawn toward each other, and other people, too, including their own children. Their worship is often dry and mechanical, dutiful, even frustrating. At times God seems to be as far from them as East is from West. And yet, such spouses have their moments, moments in which they are luminously sacramental to each other and to all who know them. In these moments, they clearly realize their ideal. The moments may at first be few and far between, but they are unmistakably real, as if the two have fallen in love all over again. And as time goes by, these moments grow. They become deeper, they come more often, they last longer. Skin-to-Skin Prime Time assures that passion comes to be, after years of slow and quiet growth, the constant state in which two lovers live, and move, and have their being.

But how do ideals become real? What exactly is the second kind of ideal, the one that is not a pipe dream but a goal, a guide for the actions which bring it into reality? Underneath the moments of luminous intimacy that we have just described, there is a deeper, more constant intimacy which flows like a river from the first moment of a couple's falling in love.

> You know, while you were at work this morning, I suddenly *realized* that we are in love, and I could hardly believe it! It's wonderful that we met each other and fell in love. That could have not happened. I could have married someone else. But I didn't. Something told me it wasn't quite right. Thanks be to God for bringing us togeth-

er! All of a sudden, I was so aware of His gift, His bringing us together, that I had to just stop what I was doing and think about it. I really am crazy about you, like I've never been before.

Such special moments make intimacy more evident, but it is really there all the time. For there is something peculiar about human ideals. They become real, really real, as soon as we take them for our goals. And they remain real as long as we keep them as goals, even if in our weakness we fail to act them out. Thus as long as a couple sincerely strive for intimacy, they achieve it. The only way in which their deeper intimacy can be ruptured is for them to make a deliberate choice to give it up. They may not always realize their passion with full awareness. But it is real all the same.

The reason why intimacy is real, even when we seem to fail and fall into confusion, selfishness, misunderstanding, and failure, is because of a psychological law: in loving, we are what we intend to be. To take a simple example, a man who tries his best to save a drowning child and fails is just as much a hero as one who succeeds. His weakness, in being overcome by physical forces that are too strong for him, does not take away one iota from his love of the child. In married life, too, a couple who try their best to achieve sexual intimacy and fail from time to time are just as intimate as if they had a more constant success. They may have misunderstandings and sexual problems, conflicts and distractions, all due to human weakness. But if they sincerely try their best to live in passionate devotion, their intimacy is real in spite of its deficiencies.

Here is where ideals of the second kind, aims or goals, differ from ideals that are romantic pipe dreams. When we have a goal in mind, it is of course just an idea in our minds at first. But once we decide to realize it as best we can, once we commit ourselves to it, we base our actions on it. Such an ideal not only *can* be real, it *is* real. When two people, then, devote themselves to becoming one with each other, they instantly become one with each other. Their intimate communion is real from that moment on, unless they deliberately choose not to be one with each other. Passion may later be clouded a bit as they become distracted by other concerns. But it is not destroyed, by any means. And when they enjoy their special moments of ecstatic realization, those moments merely reveal more clearly what was present all along.

Sexual intimacy is like a journey to a distant city. Once a couple choose it as their ideal, they take the first step along the road that leads to that destination. But they do not have to be consciously thinking of their destination every single moment in order to move toward it. Just as a driver stays on the right road even when he thinks of other things, a couple live in a very deep and real intimacy in between their special moments of awareness. And the ideal for intimacy gradually becomes more and more real as it motivates their daily actions. Once they have accepted the ideal of intimacy, they make many decisions, speak many words, carry out many actions, that would not have happened otherwise. And those decisions and actions are intimate.

One couple we know went through a period of several weeks when their plans for Prime Time were frustrated nearly every day. One or the other would get sick, or unexpected company would come. One night, severe thunderstorms came, knocking out their power and frightening their children.

The next day the wife said, "You know, I'm beginning to wonder about us. An occasional miss is o.k., but I wonder if that old bugaboo, shame, is operating to keep us apart."

"Well, I certainly don't want it to be that way," he answered.

"Neither do I," she said. "Let's keep trying."

Couples seeking intimacy have one important advantage. In many other areas of life, achievement is all that counts. If someone fails, he gets no credit for good intentions. If a baseball player strikes out, for example, he cannot plead that he meant well, that he did his best, that he should get credit for trying. In baseball, results are what count. A player who fails often enough soon finds himself out of a job, no matter how sincerely he wants to hit the ball. But in matters of human love, and of sexual intimacy, the situation is different. Good intentions do count. Any effort is automatically an achievement. Thus a couple who *desire* to be intimate *are* intimate. To desire to love is to already love. Recall our earlier definition of love: to love is to wish someone his good, for his sake. The love is in the wishing. The definition says nothing about effectively bringing about the good that we wish for our beloved. Naturally, if we sincerely wish it, we will make out best effort to bring it about. But our best effort may not be enough. We may not succeed, for many reasons beyond our control. Such failure does not take away from our love, nor from the intimacy that love produces. Lovers can make honest mistakes, and keep their intimacy intact. They can fail out of weakness, and keep their intimacy intact. They can give in to pressures, and keep their intimacy intact. For in matters of human love, every try is a success.

There is a famous short story by O. Henry, *The Gift of the Magi*, which brings out this truth. The husband, in order to buy his wife a special gift for Christmas (a comb for her beautiful long hair) sells his watch. And his wife, in order to buy him a special watch fob, has her hair cut off and sells it. Both tried, out of love, to give the best possible gift. And both failed, as they gave gifts which were totally unusable. But the honest mistakes that they made did not detract from their love. The gifts sealed their intimacy just as surely as if they had given each other something more useful. In fact, their intimacy was enhanced. Their Christmas was one of those special, luminous moments in which their intimacy was realized. It was made real, and was seen to be real, because of their love. The sacrament of matrimony guarantees love, but not success — except for the success of love itself. A husband who wishes to love does love. A wife who wishes to love also loves.

> 'Honey, now that the kids are grown, I'd like to go back to school. I'd like to get my high school diploma, and then go on to college. I'd like to get a degree in psychology.'

Marie was obviously excited as she spoke her dream to her husband. He, however, was instantly depressed. Marie wondered why.

> 'Honey, I know that money is not the problem. I've already looked at the expenses. Is something else wrong?'

Jim just continued to look glum and said nothing.

> 'You won't lose my company — I've looked at the schedule, and I can take all my classes when you are gone to work. I promise I won't let studying interfere with our time together. And I'll still do all the housework. Sweetheart, what is it? I can see you're not happy with my idea.'

Finally Jim spoke, in solemn and carefully chosen words:

> 'That would be a complete reversal of the self that you presented to me when we were married.'

Jim is somewhat unusual. He really wants dialogue, shared feelings, and intimacy with his wife. Like most American men, he was brought up to believe that men should keep their feelings to themselves, and that to admit any weakness, especially to a woman, is unmanly. And yet he does try to overcome that training and reveal his feelings to his wife. He does not always succeed, and she often feels frustrated because she does not know what he is feeling, even when he tries to tell her.

The conversation we have just quoted is a fairly typical one. Jim certainly would not say, in so many words, that he wants his wife never to change, to grow, to develop new interests. And yet, when her new interests arouse his fear and resentment, he tells her. His telling may not be wholly successful, for sharing feelings is no easy task. Perhaps he does not know his feelings very accurately. Many of us don't. Jim may not be basically resentful of his wife's new interests. He may be feeling a fear that in her changes she will stop loving him. She, of course, cannot reassure him about that fear if she does not know that he is feeling it. As their conversation ended, she felt quite frustrated. He had denied her wish to go to school. And she did not understand the feelings that lay behind his denial. Jim felt frustrated too. He had made a heroic effort towards mutual understanding, one that cost a great deal of pain to his false masculine pride, and he had failed. He began to cry because he could not satisfy his wife's desire to know his feelings.

Soon Marie began to cry, too. Such conversations were becoming more and more frequent in their home, and she was afraid of a real breakup, a rupture in their intimacy that would drive them to the divorce court. She came to us for advice. Her complaint: "He keeps telling me he will try to be better, and reveal his feelings to me. But then he doesn't do it. And so I have to think that his promises are not sincere, that he only makes them to get me off his back." Sincerity, of course, is the most important feature of human love, and of sexual intimacy. If one spouse claims to care about the other's happiness but doesn't try to see what it is, or makes only halfhearted efforts to bring it about, then we know that the claim is false. There is no real desire for intimacy, no sincere devotion to intimacy as a goal. And then there is no intimacy, either. But when a desire to love is sincere, then love is present. And when intimacy is desired as a goal, intimacy is real, whether the efforts to communicate succeed completely or not.

Our first word of advice to this couple was that Marie must believe in Jim's sincerity. A man's tears, considering what it costs a man to cry before his wife over some failure to please her, are a very strong sign of his sincerity. Marie, then, should not conclude that his promises of better verbal intimacy are false. In other words, she must trust Jim. She must believe that he loves her, that he wants deeper intimacy with her and is making a sincere effort to bring it about. And both must believe in the reality of their deep, underlying intimacy, which became real at the first moment of their decision to strive for it. All the failures in the world, all the mistakes, all the weaknesses, cannot touch that deep reality of their communion. It may take some time for it to become luminously evident to them, when they achieve the kind of communication they are striving for. But meanwhile, it is real and present as a support for their efforts. Intimacy desired is intimacy achieved.

Jim and Marie needed to use Prime Time to help each other to recall their falling in love. They needed to relive the first truly luminous moment of their intimacy. For the reality that they publicly celebrated at their wedding — their passion — was already present then, binding them in intimacy that was truly sacramental. Their wedding was their public promise to make their best effort to nurture the passion that already bound them together, so that their intimacy could grow. But notice that we said their *best* effort. Their human best effort will never be 100% successful. Both are frail, fallen human beings with many weaknesses and flaws. They will often misunderstand each other, despite their best effort to understand. They will often fail each other even when they do understand — sometimes out of weakness, sometimes out of downright selfishness. But their basic intimacy will remain, as a motive and a hope, unless they deliberately choose to give it up as their ideal, as the goal of their life together. In fact, this basic sacramental reality survives as long as even one spouse loves the other in passionate devotion. Suppose Jim becomes a complete alcoholic, or Marie abandons him for someone else. Even then, when a wronged spouse continues to love — to wish well for the other, to keep their intimacy as a goal and motive — the two will be in communion. And in that communion, the innocent one will also live in intimacy with Father, Son and Spirit.

Needless to say, the intimacy of separated spouses is not the best kind and is not luminously sacramental. It is full of darkness and pain. But a basic sexual intimacy lives in the heart of the faithful spouse, and remains as a basis for a real hope of reconciliation. The healing grace of matrimony will still be operative, and might be a strong force to bring about the repentance and return of the spouse who has been wrong. It may take heroic faith to believe in such intimacy and in the grace it brings. But the reality is there for anyone who wants to believe in it. My aunt and godmother stayed with an alcoholic husband for ten miserable years when everyone was advising her to leave him. "No," she often said, "I want to give him a chance to change." And change he did, eventually. He stopped drinking, became an active member of AA, and enjoyed a most poignant intimacy with his wife for the next thirty years. Their love, after many hard years, became an inspiration — a sacrament — for their children, their grandchildren, and everyone who knew them.

The Church's refusal to allow people to divorce and remarry does seem harsh at times, and we should keep seeking lawful ways to make it less harsh. But we must also understand the reason behind it, a very precious sacramental reality, the intimacy that can exist between a couple even when it is clouded by their problems and failures. That continuing intimacy, though dark, is a basis for reconciliation which the pagans do not have. The healing of such broken marriages can be a powerful healing grace for all in the Church, and even beyond. Intimacy is a reality which we ought not to give up on too lightly. Abused spouses may separate from their abusers, of course. But it makes a great deal of sense,in the light of faith, for them to wait — in love and in hope, to reconcile, to wait for the other's conversion and return.

Take the couple in *Kramer v. Kramer*, for example — a couple who separated because the wife needed to "find herself," and the husband wasn't helping her to do so. By the end of the picture both had learned and changed, and the problems which had led them to separate were solved. And yet the picture left them separated, presumably to search for new partners. Had they been Catholics, their sacramental sexual intimacy could well have drawn them back together. Catholic couples have a special reason to forgive and forget. And that reason is not just sociological, that society benefits from stable marriages. Nor is it merely psychological, that people are happier and more comfortable when separations are healed. The reason is sacramental. It is sexual intimacy as the healing presence of Father, Son and Spirit, that presence which endures as long as spouses try their best to love in passion and devotion.

Passion, indeed, is the key, here as in every other aspect of sacramental married life. Let us go back to Jim and Marie for a moment. When Jim refused to approve Marie's return to school, she could have done several things. She might have simply dropped the subject and given up her dreams. She might have lived out her life in suppressed resentment. Such a decision would have held back Marie's growth as a person, and that would seriously weaken their intimacy, even if it preserved a surface peace between them. It certainly would have blocked her passion for Jim. Or she might have openly defied Jim, rejected his negative feelings, and gone to school without his approval. That rejection would have seriously damaged their intimacy, too, and probably their surface peace as well. But Marie and Jim, devoted as they were to passion and intimacy as their real ideal, took the harder, more sacramental way. They chose to talk out their differences and try to resolve them, but in the context of carefully nurtured passion. It was very difficult at first for Marie to warm up sexually to a man who had declared himself opposed to one of the dreams of her life, and for no good reason that she could see. But she deliberately aroused her passion for him anyway, recalling many good points which had originally drawn her to him and believing in the sincerity of his efforts to love her even more. As she became more passionate than ever, Jim felt more reassured that her love for him was not threatened by her new interests. They had many loving conversations, painful to both of them, as they struggled for understanding and agreement. But their passion never flagged. After a couple of years, Jim's feelings were soothed, he felt secure in Marie's love and was able to send her off to school with his blessing.

This story has its funny part, too, as most human stories do. Marie soon found that she didn't really like school all that much and dropped out after a few months. But the door had been opened — permanently and peacefully — for her to continue to grow and explore her interests without her husband feeling threatened. Passion had kept their intimacy alive in spite of a temporary failure to act it out perfectly. Failures are bound to occur in the concrete details of two people living together in daily intimacy. The Church's hope of reconciling broken marriages tells us something very important about marriages that do not break up: passion preserves a deep underlying intimacy between spouses even when they may fail on the level of action and conversation. The popular movie *Love Story* promoted the theme, "Loving is never having to say you're sorry." But that message is false. Loving is often having to be sorry, and often having to say that we are. And it is often having to accept such sorrow and to forgive. The basis for forgiveness in a good marriage is the same as the basis for reconciling a broken marriage: the passion which keeps intimacy alive, and powerful, as the deep underlying current of a couple's life together.

For any human relationship to last, the people involved in it must be willing to apologize for failures, to seek and receive forgiveness. Thus, when a man first begins to verbalize his feelings to his wife, he may be terrified. Such verbalizing goes against his personal identity in a very profound way. It is contrary to his deeply ingrained idea of what it is to be a man. And for a man to cry is to give a sure sign that he is weak, effeminate, a "wimp", possibly a homosexual. A man needs great courage, indeed, to overcome this false idea of manhood in order to seek intimacy with a woman.

And so most men won't be very good at verbalizing their feelings to their wives — not at first, anyway. Jim will find it hard to know in his own mind what his feelings are. He may think he is angry when he is really frightened. He may choose the wrong words at times. And he may even lapse into his former silence from time to time, keeping his feelings bottled up. But his wife has solid reason to hope for his success, to be patient with his efforts, to forgive his lapses. For once he takes intimacy as an ideal or goal, that intimacy becomes real.

The same is true of a wife who begins to overcome her sexual inhibitions. There are many quite understandable reasons why Marie might hold back her passionate feelings. She may have been brought up to believe that strong sexual desire is unfeminine, or even sinful. She may simply be afraid of giving up control of herself and of her situation. She may just be afraid of intimacy. As she sincerely tries to change, she will make many mistakes and experience many failures. She needs time to discover her sexual feelings and responses, and to learn how to act them out. She will lapse back into her old inhibitions from time to time. But her husband will be cheered by her trying—it is, after all, an enormous compliment to him. And he will be patient with her mistakes and failures. He will be quick to forgive, hopeful of success because of his faith in the power of their underlying sexual intimacy. She, too, makes intimacy real by taking it as her ideal.

All couples, then, as long as they sincerely try to improve their passion, will live a sacramental intimacy with each other and with Father, Son and Spirit. That intimacy is their constant source of hope, a basis for forgiveness, and reason to give each other credit for good intentions. In efforts toward intimacy, failure on one level can bring success on another, deeper level. When husbands and wives make mistakes, fail out of weakness, or get caught in circumstances that inhibit their conversation and lovemaking, their intimacy may still be preserved. In fact, it might even be enhanced, just as much as it would have been if they had succeeded in saying the right words or performing the right actions. Sacramental couples are not those who live in perfect understanding, always successful lovemaking, and pure, unselfish devotion. They are those who have such intimacy as an ideal. In fact, they live in joy, because they know each other's ideals, and give each other credit for trying. Since the desire for intimacy is the beginning of intimacy, and since they see that desire in each other, they are very tolerant and compassionate toward each other, and grateful for each other's efforts to love. But these are not naive, sentimental attitudes. For in their desire to be intimate, they are intimate. They are in deep communion with each other, with the Church, and with God. Joy lasts as long as intimacy does, and intimacy lasts as long as desire does.

Thus tolerance, compassion, forgiveness, and joy mark the efforts of sacramental couples who practice Skin-to-Skin Prime Time as a technique for nurturing their passion. Couples with several small children might just laugh at the idea of their finding a half hour every day in which they can be alone together, with relaxed and rested bodies and undistracted minds. One couple we know once had four children sick with the flu all at the same time, vomiting in their beds throughout the night. The couple found themselves exhausted — not just from comforting and caring for their sick children, but from doing laundry for the third round of bed changes in one night! Such unusual situations cannot always be predicted and planned for in advance. Many couples may find that, despite their best intentions, days, perhaps weeks go by without any opportunity for them to be alone together. Such a failure may not indicate a fear of intimacy or a lack of sincerity in devotion to it. Parents can go for some days with such demands on their time and energy, and such physical and mental fatigue, that they need every spare moment just to catch up on sleep. When that is the case, they can still count on the reality of their intimacy. For it is created, and sustained, by the fact that they have Prime Time as an ideal. Then they will practice it whenever they can.

Our vision does speak, then, to ordinary people, including the traveling salesman who finds prostitutes tempting. A man whose heart and mind are constantly filled with the mental picture of his wife has no problems with fidelity. When that mental picture is reinforced with memories of many, many sessions of Prime Time, naked in her arms, basking in her praise and affection, the thought of embracing another woman will simply be impossible to him. Nor will his beloved, left at home by his travels, find loneliness and boredom a problem. For she will have memories, too, and the feelings that memories generate. Prime Time will so strengthen her self-esteem, her passion for her husband, and her joy in his constant presence, that anyone else's company will pale by comparison. And sustaining them both will be their steady vision of the future that they are aiming at in their ideal of holy sex. Having taken intimacy as their goal-ideal, they look forward to the day when they will have mastered the delicate language of sexual intercourse, and have learned to share their inner selves in words. They will trust each other to continue to try, to give up defenses, and to budget time and money for a very powerful technique to create an ongoing, passionate vulnerability. And underneath it all they will be joyful in their belief that in and through their intimacy they grow in intimacy with Father, Son, and Spirit — an intimacy that will one day blossom fully into eternal life:

> And eternal life is this: to know you, the only true God, and Jesus Christ, Whom you have sent. (Jn. 17:3)

A romantic, utopian, unrealistic vision? Not unless the vision of Jesus Christ is also romantic, unrealistic and utopian. For it is He Who came that we might have life, and have it more abundantly. It is He Who commanded that we love each other as He has loved us. It was He Who said that if we keep His commandment to love, He and His Father will come to live in us. And it was He Who said that by our love for each other, all men will know that we are His disciples. For married people, sex is that life in greater abundance. Sex is the way to love as Jesus does. Sex is the way to show all men that we are His disciples. And sex — the total passionate intimacy that is the theme of this book — begins to be real in the moment when a couple first take it as their ideal, and try to live that ideal in their daily life. For the desire to love is love already, and so is the effort to love. The desire for intimacy is intimacy's beginning, and the effort toward intimacy makes it real at once.

It is most important, then, that spouses judge each other by this ideal, and not by the words and actions which fall short of it. Maurice Blondel once observed that we humans judge our own achievements by our ideals, but judge other people's ideals by their achievements. We give ourselves credit for good intentions, while we criticize the failings of others. Such a critical and self-righteous spirit is one of the effects of original sin, and is deadly to all kinds of human intimacy. But in sacramental marriages, where sex is the goal and Skin-to-Skin Prime Time a practiced technique, that sinful tendency is reversed. It is healed by the sacramental grace of intimacy. Intimate spouses then judge each other by their ideal, by their goal of sexual intimacy. The fact that they do not achieve it perfectly and all at once does not dampen their passion for each other. Instead, they accept each other's good intentions and best efforts, they overlook mistakes and weaknesses, and they forgive faults. But most of all, they live in a deep gratitude to each other for the invitation to take part in such an awesome ideal.

And then their moments of realization come, moments when they discover and realize a passionate intimacy that is beyond orgasm, and beyond any words. That intimacy, their passionate personal presence to each other and to God, is like the ecstasy that the great mystics speak of in the higher states of prayer. In such moments, the realization of one person's presence to another cannot be put into words. It simply leaves us staring at each other in an utterly silent awe. Such deep, calm realization of each other would be spoiled by any words, any activity. Even breathing seems a distraction.

Such moments are times of the deepest marital prayer. Sexual intercourse is often the way to them, but not always. Intercourse happens without such realization, and the realization often comes without intercourse. Those moments come, in fact, as a gift, a gift of the Spirit which we cannot command. But we can provide the climate for their coming. That climate is sex — the passionate presence by which spouses who aim at intimacy as their ideal, and honor each other for that ideal, live constantly in each other's minds and hearts.